West McLaren Mercedes

teamwork

THE BIOGRAPHY OF THE FORMULA 1 TEAM

West McLaren Mercedes

teamwork

THE BIOGRAPHY OF THE FORMULA 1 TEAM

Gerald Donaldson

MBI Publishing Company

MBI Publishing Company books are also available at
discounts in bulk quantity for industrial or sales-
promotional use. For details write to Special Sales Manager
at Motorbooks International Wholesalers & Distributors,
729 Prospect Avenue, Po Box 1, Osceola,
WI 54020-0001 USA.

Library of Congress Cataloging-in-Publication
Data Available.

ISBN 0-7603-0647-8

Designed and produced by Cooling Brown
Hampton, Middlesex, UK

Printed in Italy

contents

foreword

IT TOOK SOME TIME for me to become convinced that this book should be written. My reservations were based partly on a concern that capturing the true nature of our complex organization and the way it operates would be very difficult to achieve accurately and fairly between the covers of a book. There was also some reluctance to permit an outsider, even an author of high-quality books about our sport, to move freely within the team. Yet such freedom would be the only way a work of this nature could be successfully undertaken. A more distant view would lack perspective and objectivity. What ultimately led to my approval being given for the project to proceed was the author's stated intention of focusing on the heart of the team – and the key to its success – its people. Once that objective was established, Gerald Donaldson was granted our full co-operation and given complete access to our organization.

While engaged in his research, Gerald observed us closely over two racing seasons, a period of time that coincided with the team's dramatic return to winning form. The human component accompanying that technical achievement makes compelling reading. Inevitably, we also experienced some setbacks. These, too, are well-documented, and both the pleasure and the pain inherent in our sport are depicted with feeling.

teamwork affords deep insights into our organization and it is pleasing to note that recognition is given to the important contributions made by everyone in the team, not just those in the public eye. This most vital aspect of the way we work makes the title of the book particularly apt.

On a personal note, though they make me feel good, certain passages in the book I find somewhat embarrassing. Nonetheless, on balance, I believe that Gerald has realized his goal. By talking to so many of our people, and through his own observations, the book shows how our team works, and reveals its essential character and distinctive personality. Everyone is fiercely proud of being part of the company, and I am no exception. I hope that in reading **teamwork** you will have an insight into that depth of pride and the profound emotion all of us feel about McLaren International and the West McLaren Mercedes team.

RON DENNIS

Managing Director – The TAG McLaren Group

introduction

IN FORMULA 1 RACING the famous drivers in the exotic cars are understandably the main focus of attention. But what is seen on the Grand Prix circuits around the world is only the highly visible tip of the proverbial iceberg: a huge mass of ice floating in the sea with much the greater part under water. Beneath the surface of the sea of thrilling racing are the teams behind the scenes that are the foundation of the sport. The job they have to do is defined in the word 'teamwork': the combined effort of organized co-operation by a group of people working together for a common cause.

In this sport the common cause is trying to win in a fiercely competitive environment. F1 is often compared to warfare, with the teams engaged in all-out combat on race tracks that are battlefields. The military analogy is apt considering that the teams, armed to the teeth with highly sophisticated technological weaponry, are composed of highly trained armies of skilled personnel who must maintain rigid discipline while facing a continual barrage of distraction and danger. The F1 soldiers on the firing line are led by a chain of command that must keep its head under

a relentless bombardment of pressure to succeed. Backing up the troops is a complex infrastructure that must deal with a wide array of organizational and logistical problems, not the least of which is transporting the army to far-flung war zones.

On a more peaceful note, an F1 team is in reality an automobile manufacturer, creating and producing its own racing cars, a hugely expensive proposition that requires a team also to engage in a marketing exercise, to generate the necessary budget to fight the good fight. The attraction for investors in an F1 team is the vast international media exposure, particularly on television, which the pinnacle of motorsport can provide. Since the amount of exposure

The split-second precision of a pit stop is teamwork personified...

depends on the success of the team, with far more attention paid to frontrunners than backmarkers, the bottom line for all concerned is winning races. And in the final analysis it is superior teamwork that wins the most races.

...as masked men make minutely choreographed moves that seem balletic.

At no time during a Grand Prix is the essence of teamwork more exemplified than during a pit stop, when the pit crew springs into action in a desperate race against time. In those frantic few seconds – fraught with danger and drama, when the combined effort of organized co-operation by a group of people working for a common cause is stressed to the maximum – races can be won or lost. When duty calls, the pit crew works with split-second precision, executing minutely choreographed moves that seem as balletic as they are purposeful.

The F1 car peels off the circuit and comes howling down the pit lane, its driver homing in on the lollipop, the round board on the end of a long pole. The lollipop bears the message 'Brake' and the driver does just that, stopping to the centimetre, placing the car's four wheels precisely on the positions marked on the tarmac. The driver selects neutral, keeps the engine idling and sits in the cockpit straining with impatience, though he knows his team-mates won't keep him long. The time required to fully service his car – to replace all four Bridgestone tyres mounted on Enkei wheels, to pump 70 litres of Mobil Unleaded Performance fuel into the tank – will scarcely give the driver time to catch his breath.

The crew swarms over the gleaming grey MP4/13 chassis – its AP brakes red hot, its V10 Mercedes F0110G engine sizzling and crackling. In their jet black helmets and flameproof suits the pit crew personnel look darkly sinister and strangely anonymous. But they're not – their names and nicknames are inscribed in white letters on their black helmets.

The man with the lollipop is nicknamed Ruby. On the front and rear jacks are Ian and ATB. Señor Jo stands by to clean the driver's helmet and visor. The jackmen raise the car. At each corner the four groups of wheelmen work feverishly, replacing the used rubber in a blur of activity. Among them are Simoni, Wimp, Johnny O, Al, Trevooor, Lofty, Taff, Shadwell, Gromit, Bruv, Wingnut and Turbo. They work three to a wheel: one to operate the airgun to unscrew and tighten the central wheelnut, one to whip off the wheel and one to slap on its replacement. A raised right arm signals the millisecond each wheel is finished. When the last arm is raised, Ruby reverses the lollipop to signal 'First Gear' to the driver. The jacks are lowered. About four seconds have elapsed.

Standing by the refuelling rig are Drew, with his trusty fire extinguisher at the ready, and Bass, poised to mop up any fuel spill. Beside them, monitoring the fuel flow and ready instantly to activate the 'dead man's handle' (the emergency shut-off valve) is Red. Holding and helping guide the heavy fuel hose that writhes like an angry anaconda as pressurized fuel whooshes through it at a rate of 12 litres per second is Patch. The nozzleman, who has locked the 45kg nozzle and hose assembly onto an adapter on the fuel tank on the side of the car, is Forklift. Inside their helmets, Patch and Forklift each have a self-contained breathing apparatus in case the whole nerve-wracking, gut-wrenching exercise should suddenly go explosively wrong. But it hasn't yet for this team, and when Forks removes the nozzle Ruby withdraws the lollipop and the refettled car screams away down the pit lane in a cloud of blue tyre smoke to rejoin the race. It has been stationary for less than eight seconds.

Such a pit stop, accomplished nine-tenths of a second faster than the job done on the rival car that was leading the race, brought victory at the 1997 Italian Grand Prix – and the team was overjoyed. On one rare occasion, at the 1998 French Grand Prix, an equipment malfunction during a pit stop caused an agonizing delay that put one of the cars out of frontrunning contention – and the team despaired.

This is F1 racing. This is teamwork. All for one – for Mika and for David – and one for all – for Ron and Tats and the 60 people at the race, for Tinker and the Wrinklies and the 260 people back at base – for everyone in the West McLaren Mercedes team.

All for one, and one for all. Teamwork. In eight seconds flat.

the

home team

"While standing as testimony to McLaren's past achievements, these cars provide a constant reminder of what Formula 1 is all about: the development of technology, the human dedication, the relentless pursuit of excellence, and the successes they bring."

RON DENNIS
(on the display of cars at headquarters)

headquarters

In a business park in Woking, Surrey, stands a discreet slate-grey building faced with smoked glass windows. High on the building's right front corner, in red letters, the TAG McLaren logo identifies these premises as the team headquarters. Inside the front doors the decor of the reception area is quietly futuristic and the atmosphere reminiscent of an upmarket art gallery.

In the front lobby, behind a curved stainless steel desk on which a sculpted vase is filled with freshly cut flowers, two designer-dressed women greet a steady stream of visitors and answer a battery of constantly ringing telephones. On the right, inset in a wall that extends up into an atrium, a series of steering wheels from McLaren cars is displayed in backlit glass cases. Behind the reception desk, beside a staircase that curves up to a second level, is a tower in which an arrangement of helmets worn by McLaren drivers is stacked in more backlit glass cases. The names on the helmets are Bruce McLaren, James Hunt, Alain Prost, Ayrton Senna, Mika Hakkinen and David Coulthard.

Denise Burgess and Marjory Conlen are two of the 300-plus people in McLaren International Limited, the company that fields the racing team.

To the left of the entrance lobby, behind a wall of glass, is a long rectangular room in the foreground housing several plush grey leather sofas and chairs. In the centre of the room at the back, suspended from the ceiling are four full-size racing cars, hung like mobile sculptures to convey the impression of speed. The display of cars, as driven by Denny Hulme, Johnny Rutherford (in IndyCars), Ayrton Senna and David Coulthard, is a monument to McLaren's four decades of racing competition around the world. The success of the team's cars and drivers is also commemorated in the room. Extending from floor to ceiling along one glass-fronted wall is an artful array of some of the more than 350 trophies won by the team over the years.

On the opposite wall, two large decorative panels provide insights into the performance capabilities of the modern Formula 1 cars. The highest speed of the 1997 season, recorded by Mika Hakkinen's West McLaren Mercedes at Monza, was 353 kilometres per hour. On each lap of that circuit the car was on full throttle 70 per cent of the time. At the 1997 Canadian Grand Prix, David Coulthard's car accelerated from standstill to 100kph in 2.3 seconds, and from standstill to 200kph in 5.0 seconds. On that circuit, where the six-speed gearbox of the car was required to make 48 gear changes per lap, there were 3312 gear changes over the race distance.

Also revealed on these wall panels is some of the philosophy that is the driving force behind McLaren. A stream of buzzwords reads 'leading edge business lifestyle success leadership focus design global dynamic excellence innovation performance integrity success responsive competitive partnership technology delivery competitive teamwork'.

The display of real racing cars in the art gallery of a reception area is a reminder that McLaren's 6225 square metre headquarters facility is a working factory, where the cars are designed, built and serviced. It is also used as an office complex from where the team's business is conducted. Further confirmation that this is the heart of the team comes with a look inside, where an impressive number of people swarm around in a beehive of activity that has the place buzzing from dawn to dusk, often 24 hours a day, nearly every day of the year.

The display of some of the cars and trophies in the reception area commemorates four decades of racing success around the world.

Upstairs, a mezzanine level at the front of the building contains the administration, management and design offices. Spread out below is the factory, a purposeful labyrinth of workshops and laboratories separated by glassed-in partitions. But there are no real barriers in these brightly lit, spotlessly clean, grey-hued premises. A sense of spaciousness prevails, as does an aura of efficient informality. Everywhere the corridors of power are short and doors tend to be kept open. People are known by their first names, and most of those names are inscribed on their work uniforms, should anyone

fail immediately to connect a face with a name – a distinct possibility since McLaren International Limited, the company that fields the West McLaren Mercedes F1 team, has 320 employees. The personnel are divided into two unofficial groups: the Race Team, which includes the Test Team and the approximately 60 people who travel to the races, and the Home Team.

organization

McLaren International Limited is part of the TAG McLaren Group, which has over 750 employees and is growing all the time. Included in the Group are TAG McLaren Marketing Services Limited (about 30 people), TAG Electronic Systems Limited (which has 120 people, with a further 80 employed by TAG McLaren Audio, a recently acquired hi-fi company) and McLaren Cars Limited (140 people). These latter three enterprises are located elsewhere in the business park near the main McLaren building. In fact, the ever-expanding Group now occupies 16 buildings. These will finally be located under one roof in a new technology centre – currently being designed by the distinguished architect Sir Norman Foster and developed under the direction of TAG McLaren Holdings Limited – shortly after the turn of the century.

"Everyone is part of the team, and everyone is challenged to be successful and take pride in everything they do."

Each company within the Group is composed of different divisions and managed by a chain of command that starts with Ron Dennis, who became managing director of the TAG McLaren Group in 1997. Until that time, Ron's official title was Managing Director of McLaren International, a position that is now held by the former operations director, Martin Whitmarsh.

When Martin Whitmarsh was brought into McLaren by Ron in 1989, it was to help organize into a more manageable structure a company that had grown by leaps and bounds and, flushed with success, was threatening to run off madly in all directions – like a team of highly spirited horses. In order to harness all that potentially wayward energy, one of the first things Martin had to do was convince the man in charge to ease up on the reigns.

'When we had our first discussions,' Martin recalls, 'even before I joined the company, I got the impression Ron wasn't the delegating sort. I sensed he would have difficulty letting go and, sure enough, I was amazed to find he was still holding the lollipop during the pit stops! He explained to me how important the job was, the weight of the responsibility, and if someone were to make a mistake at such a critical time it should be him. This was in the late eighties and in those days we didn't have a trackside team manager, so Ron was effectively doing that as well. He had been lecturing me on the importance of delegating authority so as to free yourself to be able to take a strategic overview. But you can't take a strategic overview of what's going on if you leave the pit wall and sprint across to get involved in the adrenaline rush of holding the lollipop.'

Eventually, Martin persuaded Ron to let go of the lollipop, though he maintains (like everyone else) that 'what McLaren is today is very much a consequence of Ron's vision and drive'.

Martin's next job was to set up a structure that would make the team more efficient. To this task he brought the enlightenment of 10 years' experience gained first as a structural analyst, then as a manufacturing director, with British Aerospace. While F1 is closely associated with the automotive industry, the production of racing cars is also linked to the aerospace industry. In each case, Martin notes, there is one important difference: 'Here, the pace of development and manufacture is mind-blowingly quicker.'

To accommodate the heady pace of F1, to encourage and not stifle the creative quick thinking necessary to best flourish in such short time frames, requires keeping bureaucracy to a minimum. For Martin this delicate balancing act of implementing 'systemization and control at McLaren still makes me nervous every time we do it. I'm very cautious and conscious of the fact that the degree of responsiveness and accountability we have is exceptionally high.'

"Nowadays it's unlikely that there is a genius around who has the technical capability, talent and knowledge, let alone the time, to be better than the summation of a group of experts."
Martin Whitmarsh

Martin Whitmarsh, managing director of McLaren International, has organized into a more manageable structure a company that has grown by leaps and bounds.

It is also part of Martin's job to account for the money it costs to run the team, though his view that 'I'm probably perceived as the miser in the organization!' is tempered by the fact that 'we have the luxury of being incredibly well financed. But the money doesn't just come pouring in willy nilly. As a business we've gone out and sold ourselves, presented ourselves well and generated the budget we need to do the job. Of course, the more money you have the higher the expectations. Though, I must say, we are blessed with shareholders who are not simply interested in the pursuit of wealth and a quick return on their investments.'

The TAG Group, a company established in 1977 by the late Saudi Arabian entrepreneur Akram Ojjeh, has been a major shareholder in McLaren since 1985. TAG is an acronym for Techniques d'Avant Garde (advanced technology). Besides the companies within the TAG McLaren Group, its diversified business interests includes real estate, property management and hotel development (in France, Sardinia and the USA), high-tech farming (in California), custom-built utility vehicles (based in Switzerland) and aviation (distributing executive jets, leasing charter aircraft, and manufacturing aircraft components).

Ron Dennis, managing director of TAG McLaren Group, with his friend and business partner Mansour Ojjeh, chairman of the TAG Group of companies.

The TAG Group is a major shareholder in TAG Heuer SA, a recently floated company renowned as makers of precision timepieces and also the official F1 timekeeper since 1992. The TAG Group is now headed by Mansour Ojjeh, son of the founder. A close friend of Ron Dennis, Mansour Ojjeh is also chairman of the TAG McLaren Group.

Says Martin Whitmarsh: 'We have a situation where Ron and Mansour want us to succeed. They want us to win races. They want us to win championships. They want us to do it with style. They want us to do it with the right organization that has the

right: **Mansour Ojjeh.**

right culture, the right people, the right ethos, throughout the company. That ethos is based on a belief that every detail matters. We want to build the best race car but we also want to have the best company restaurant, the cleanest floors in the industry. The people here who make the tea and clean the factory contribute to the welfare of the people who contribute to the welfare of the business.

'Everyone is part of the team, and everyone is challenged to be successful and take pride in everything they do. I think this leads to common traits in our people, because people are influenced by the team environment. They all have individual personalities, but the way they perform and react to situations and circumstances is also a consequence of the conditioning that happens when they work here. When you have the right people organized in the right way, you have a remarkably strong team.

'The popular view of motor racing is that races are won and lost at the track. And they often are, but my view is that we send out a product – which is the package of a car and support equipment – for a highly competent race team to go to the track and exploit that product to its limit. But the limit is largely predetermined by the product – by what gets loaded onto the transporters here at the factory.'

Jo Ramirez, team co-ordinator. His passionate love for racing has kept him involved since 1962.

Martin explains how McLaren International is divided into four main sections that, respectively, 'look after the money, design and develop the car, make the car and operate the car'. These sections, as shown on Martin's comprehensive Organization Chart, are headed by Bob Illman (Financial Director), Adrian Newey (Technical Director), Geoff Highley (Head of Manufacturing) and Dave Ryan (Race Team Manager).

Approximately a dozen people work in administration, which includes an accounting department and a legal department with a resident lawyer. There is also a travel department, headed by Jo Ramirez. His title is Team Co-ordinator and his job covers a myriad of details that must be dealt with on a daily basis. Jo, who was born in Mexico City, has been involved in F1 racing for over three decades,

teamwork · **the home team**

giving him a wealth of on-the-job experience and a first-hand knowledge of the nomadic life many F1 people lead.

Jo began as a 'gofer' (go for this, go for that) for Ferrari, doing odd jobs for the team and one of its drivers, his friend and countryman, Ricardo Rodriguez. Jo was devastated when Ricardo was killed in 1962 at their home race in Mexico City, but his love of racing – 'the look of the cars, the sound of the engines, the smell of the fuel and the tyres' – kept him in the sport. Jo worked as an apprentice mechanic for Lamborghini in Italy, then moved to England to become a mechanic for Ford's sportscar team. He was a mechanic on Dan Gurney's Eagle F1 team when it won its first race in 1967, and during his tenure as a mechanic at Tyrrell the team won 11 Grands Prix. From 1975 to 1983 he was team manager for the Copersucar, Shadow, ATS and Theodore F1 teams.

In the early seventies Jo met Ron Dennis, who was working for the Brabham team. He was a man who seemed destined for a bright future, as Jo remembers. 'Anybody who knew Ron at that time thought he would go places because he was a very energetic, electric young man. He never stood still and was always trying to make things better.'

When Ron went on to form his own racing teams, several times he invited Jo to work for him. Though they remained friends and played squash together, it wasn't until 1984 that Jo joined McLaren to become co-ordinator for the team, which had only 60 employees at the time. Nowadays, that many people go to the races, and the responsibilities of Jo and those who work with him include looking after the organization and logistics of travel arrangements for both the Test and Race Teams to circuits around the world.

Jo and his team of travel specialists book nearly 1500 hotel rooms (for staff and guests), 675 return flights (amounting to annual distances of over 150,000 kilometres per person), hire cars and so on. They also look after shipping the equipment – fuel, engines, supplies – which for 'flyaway' races amounts to a total weight of 20,000 kilograms. Besides the three racing cars for the races outside

"The thing about McLaren is the high level of grit and determination. It's a very long-established team with a very stable workforce."

Europe, they also arrange the shipment of some 115 flight cases (including Jo's, since he travels with the Race Team). At each Grand Prix Jo performs a wide variety of tasks. His duties keep him so busy there seems little time in his life for much other than work. But he loves what he does and, in fact, he doesn't even call it work.

'I think there are few people in this world who have something they love so much that is also their job. I've always said that the first time I get up in the morning and say "Oh, I have to go to work", then that's the time I will stop. But that has never happened. So I'm lucky that my job is my passion. You'll find a lot of people like that here.'

engineering While Jo Ramirez is a veteran McLaren man, Adrian Newey is a recent arrival, filling a new role as the team's technical director. Adrian joined McLaren late in the 1997 season from Williams where a succession of championship-winning cars earned him a reputation as one of the very best F1 designers.

right: **Adrian Newey, technical director. As a boy he built scale model cars. Now, he is regarded as one of the very best F1 designers.**

The seeds for his future profession were sewn early in Adrian's life when his father, a vet and a motoring enthusiast, bought Lotus Elans in kit form and assembled them into road-going vehicles. As a boy Adrian also built scale model F1 cars from kits, and from the beginning he was more interested in engineering than driving. When he discovered kart racing, aged 13, he quickly became an expert in welding and tuning the rudimentary chassis and rebuilding the engines. His father agreed to contribute equally to his racing campaign, but this was 'fairly under-financed' since Adrian's share came from the meagre income earned from his newspaper route. However, budget limitations dampened neither his enthusiasm nor his technical passion and at 15 Adrian designed an electronic ignition system.

After a brief flirtation with motorbikes, Adrian concentrated on scholastically equipping himself for what was now his goal in life: a career in motor racing. Armed with a degree in Aeronautical Engineering from Southampton University he approached several F1 teams and was accepted by Emerson Fittipaldi's Copersucar team. He later went to March Engineering where he developed cars that won

championships in the American-based IndyCar series, then came back into F1 with the Leyton House team before joining Williams in 1990. He came to McLaren in search of a new challenge.

'The thing about McLaren,' Adrian notices, 'is the high level of grit and determination. It's obviously a very long-established team with a very stable workforce. They've been working with each other for a long time and they've gained each other's respect. They're very highly motivated, very professional, with a collective work ethic that's brought about by the individuals. If you look in the drawing offices, for instance, everything is very disciplined. People come in here in the morning, have a quick chat for five minutes, then get on with it.'

Adrian acknowledges that McLaren's reputation for having such a highly developed work ethic contributes to a perception that the team is so seriously strait-laced that its personnel are dull, cold and humourless.

'But I don't think that's true at all. They are hard working but I don't think they are rigid and they certainly aren't dull. I've been very impressed by the warmth, friendliness and camaraderie, and how little there is in the way of politics inside the team. So often in teams you see one department having a go at another department, or within a department people don't get on with each other. And so you get these sort of political power struggles, which are obviously very destructive and undermine the whole effort. There is remarkably little of that in McLaren and this is another attraction.'

Of course, as a racing enthusiast, the main attraction for Adrian Newey is applying his technical expertise to the business of creating cars for competition. 'That's where the main enjoyment is. It has the creative side of really starting with a clean sheet of paper, working with all the other engineers here, to create a car. It has the research areas and it has the trackside element of trying to get the best out of the car. At the end of the day, what we're judged on is how well we perform at the races. In '96 I was race engineer for Damon [Hill] (when he won the Championship with Williams) and greatly enjoyed it. This job has a lot of facets to it and I find that variety very stimulating.'

As McLaren's technical director, Adrian is responsible for four main engineering functions: Vehicle Technology (led by Chief Engineer, Paddy Lowe), Aerodynamics (Chief Engineer, Henri Durand), Vehicle Design (Chief Designer, Neil Oatley) and Race Engineering (headed by Steve Hallam). Each of these divisions is further subdivided, so that Paddy Lowe's Vehicle Technology department includes Embedded Systems (the computers on the car), Computer Simulation (whereby the cars are effectively 'raced' on computers to study their performance), Vehicle Dynamics (research and development) and Future Projects.

Steve Nichols, head of Future Projects and also a successful amateur racing driver, talks shop with David Coulthard.

Vehicle Dynamics, which was formed in the late eighties (and known then as R&D), is now headed by Tim Goss and uses five main facilities: a materials laboratory (to evaluate the materials used to make the car), a structural test centre (which contains the 'four poster' – a test rig that can accommodate a full-size car, and subject it to the stresses and strains of individual Grand Prix circuits), a wind tunnel (located at nearby Teddington, to assess the car's aerodynamic performance), an instrumentation and electronics area (where data from the cars is collected, analysed and interpreted) and a hydraulics 'clean room' (where hydraulic actuators, suspension dampers, pumps and sub-assemblies are built and tested).

Peter Hodgman, who joined McLaren as a mechanic over 20 years ago and is now laboratory manager in Vehicle Dynamics, notes that F1 these days 'is all about research and development, squeezing those few vital fractions of a second out of the car without compromising the safety of the driver. New materials, new designs and new technology all have a role to play, but it's up to us to make it happen.'

While much of Vehicle Technology is concerned with more immediate matters, the Future Projects section looks further down the road and the man who heads it is eminently qualified to take this perspective. Steve Nichols was born in Salt Lake City, Utah, and first became interested in F1 racing when he read about the 1962 season in an American racing magazine. After graduating in Mechanical Engineering from the University of Utah, Steve went to work for Hercules, the aerospace company that first supplied the carbon fibre for McLaren's pioneering chassis using that material. He then went to Gabriel, designing dampers for IndyCars. Steve found the work rewarding, but there was a faraway look in his eyes.

'I still remember being at the IndyCar races on some weekends where there would be a Formula 1 race on the television at the hotel. I would be looking at it and thinking "that is where I have got to be". It always held a huge fascination for me. I was attracted from the point of view that I was at that time racing karts myself, so I liked the driving aspect, but I also liked the devices and the competition factor. It was the combination of the athleticism of the drivers and the sophistication of the cars that was so enticing.'

And so Steve came to F1, beginning with McLaren in 1981 and continuing until the end of the 1989 season. After a five-year sojourn at Ferrari, Sauber and Jordan, he returned to McLaren. Over the years he has assumed a variety of roles in the team. The one he remembers most fondly was playing a major part in creating the team's most successful car, the 1988 MP4/4, and working with its most successful driver.

'That was probably the most satisfying period in my career. It was my responsibility to look after the design and throughout 1988 I was continuing to develop that car, but also I was Ayrton Senna's race engineer. In the end Ayrton won his first World Championship, so the combination of designing the car, then running it and working with Ayrton was really quite satisfying. Much has been said about Ayrton but, very briefly, he was extremely good. He was very warm and very giving and wanted to share the experience with you. He was always letting you know how much he appreciated your help and your efforts. This is a very tough business and when you can have good relationships like that and get good results it's immensely rewarding.

'Formula 1 is a continuous difficult challenge and I quite like that. I like a job where it matters if you do it right. If you screw up you know about it; if you do it right you know about it – immediately – which doesn't happen in other jobs. I quite enjoy having the pressure on. It's a bit like walking along the edge of a cliff, I suppose. I am a little bit afraid of heights, yet it is exciting and stimulating to look over the edge. There's a great feeling of satisfaction in this business, where you have that tremendous pressure that brings you right to the edge, and when you have done well and you haven't fallen off, that's very rewarding. Quite a high state of awareness and nervous energy are necessary to elevate your performance, tempered with a calm, rational approach. It's a good feeling.'

If this sounds more like a racing driver than an engineer, it may have something to do with that fact that Steve Nichols also races cars, and quite successfully. In 1997 he won six of the 12 FF2000 races he entered.

aerodynamics
To the uninitiated most single-seater racing cars look very similar, but to those intimately involved with them, especially their creators, they are as individual as people – or sheep. 'We are like shepherds minding a flock of sheep and are able to instantly recognize even a slight difference or particular characteristic.'

This is Henri Durand, head of Aerodynamics, the department where the specific characteristics that make up the shape of the car are determined. Born in France, Henri came to McLaren in 1990, after working for three years at Ferrari. While he is primarily concerned with aerodynamics (the interaction between airflow and the movement of an F1 car through the air), Henri is also very aware of the importance of extracting the maximum performance from the characteristics of the 18 people who interact in the department he created.

Henri Durand, head of Aerodynamics, is from France, one of several countries represented in the team's workforce.

'I would say my primary goal is to ensure that I extract 100 per cent of their potential. My secondary goal, but with the same importance, is to extract 100 per cent of my

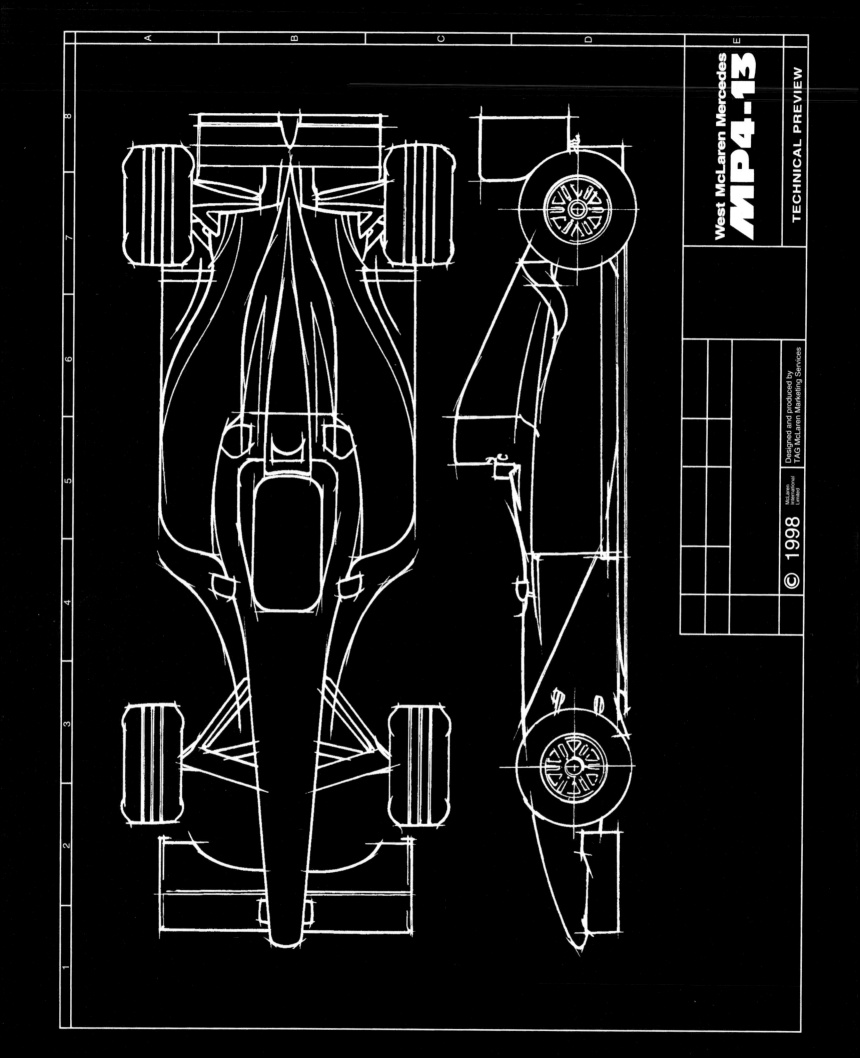

own potential, as a base. I think it is a combination of these two that makes me enjoy my work. Generally, the items we produce rarely make history. What remains at the end, the inheritance of what you have done, is effectively the structure – the technology and facility, and especially the people.

'I think the most comfortable thing about McLaren is that you've got everything you need to perform to 100 per cent of your potential. I think the general impression you have if you wander around our drawing office is that you see people very focused on their work. The environment is excellent. The company is very well structured, very well organized, with a very understanding management. It starts at the top level. Our managing director gives us the drive. He has spent so much energy in supplying the employees with the right tools and the right environment for them to perform.'

Once Henri and his team have created initial aerodynamic concepts – in the form of schematic Computer Aided Design (CAD) designs – they are then realized three dimensionally by means of 40 per cent scale model cars that are built in the factory by six full-time model makers, then put through their paces in the wind tunnel at Teddington. There, the 2.1 metre long, 30 kilogramme models are tested from seven in the morning until eight at night, with up to 2000 test runs used to develop one car.

Once the aerodynamic parameters are established the mechanical design of the car commences, which brings Neil Oatley's Vehicle Design department into the picture.

design
Neil Oatley, the team's chief designer since 1989, is described by Martin Whitmarsh as 'just an incredible enthusiast, and if you go into his home there will be walls and walls of motor racing books and memorabilia. He's a very, very quiet individual and his attention to detail is just fantastic. Neil is absolutely, tremendously McLaren.'

left: **Drawings of the 1998 F1 car.** *right:* **Neil Oatley is chief designer. One of his boyhood heroes was the founder of the team, Bruce McLaren.**

The 2.1 metre long, 30kg models are tested from seven in the morning until eight at night, with up to 2000 test runs used to develop one car.

Neil Vernon Oatley was born in London then moved close to the Brands Hatch circuit in Kent, where he often went on race weekends. One of his boyhood heroes was Bruce McLaren, who was both an F1 driver and an engineer, and it was the latter occupation that most interested Neil. 'I always wanted to be a race car designer, even from my early teenage years. Luckily enough, the things I was good at academically all dovetailed into the sort of career I've got now.'

With his degree in Automotive Engineering from Loughborough University, Neil started as a draftsman with Williams in 1977 and progressed from race engineer to design engineer. It is the creative design aspect of engineering that has always most intrigued Neil. He is an admirer of the work of Isambard Kingdom Brunel, the innovative British Victorian engineer noted for designing bridges, railways and steamships, and Charles Rennie Mackintosh, the architect who, Neil says, 'produced buildings and interiors of high aesthetic quality and timelessness'.

right: **Composite technicians cut, trim and weave sheets of carbon fibre over moulds in staggered layers to form the bodywork.**

Neil's personal appreciation of the artistic side of engineering, he believes, is also shared by those he works with. 'I think everybody at McLaren always appreciates a nice part of the car, even if it's something the public can't see. If it's pleasing to the eye, well made and well thought out, as well as functional, it adds to the pleasure everyone has in making and creating the car.'

There are a lot of parts to take pleasure from – 5000 to 6000 of them in each chassis. Neil's Vehicle Design department produces from 1700 to 1800 drawings for the components of a new chassis, and 700 to 800 more drawings are necessary for the manufacturing process. Under Neil's guidance a team of about 20 designers works in four groups, each one headed by a project leader and with specific responsibilities for one-quarter of the car: chassis, suspension, transmission and engine installation.

With so many people putting so much of themselves into the design of the car, there is an understandably high level of anticipation when it is time to put the results of their labour to the ultimate test.

As Neil Oatley says: 'The period it takes to design a car is really about five to six months, from when you start the initial drawings to when the car finally appears. I think in a lot of cases you know the first day the car runs whether it's going to be an uphill struggle, or if you're just about there and need only to keep chiselling away to be competitive. So it's a very emotional moment and always a tremendous relief when it looks good "right out of the box".'

But before the car is put into 'the box' it must be built, and that process takes place in the factory workshops where the components are manufactured and assembled into the finished product.

On Martin Whitmarsh's Organization Chart for McLaren International the most names are found under the heading Workshops and Services, the section of the factory run by Geoff Highley, head of Manufacturing. Martin calls Geoff 'probably the biggest "employer" in the company. He looks after Production, which includes buying, inspection, electrical and assembly. Then there is the Pattern Shop, Composites, the Machine Shop, Fabrication, Transport, Factory Services and Catering.'

production

Each department under the heading of Workshops and Services is run by a manager, such as Ray Grant, the veteran McLaren employee who is production control manager. Working as a supervisor in the Assembly division of Production is Gary Walker who, like Ray, also worked as a mechanic on the Race Team. Gary, with experience as Number One mechanic for both Alain Prost and Ayrton Senna from 1988 to 1992, knows a thing or two about real racing cars, though he now also makes 'dummy' ones.

'The car is a highly complex piece of engineering,' Gary acknowledges, 'and although every department works very closely to develop the finished product we are the linchpin that ultimately brings all their efforts together. The vast majority of components we receive are hand crafted, and although they are produced to the highest specifications, even the smallest change in tolerance can affect the final construction process.'

So Gary and his workmates begin with a 'dinosaur', a full-size wooden mock-up of the chassis monocoque, built by the Pattern Shop and the sub-assembly team to replicate the design of the various components and make sure the pieces of the puzzle fit together exactly. Once everything works in wood the components enter the manufacturing process, after which they are put together into a 'proper' car by the Assembly team.

pattern shop

Many components begin life in the Pattern Shop, where Manager Mick East and his eight trusty craftsmen build accurate replicas from which precision moulds are taken to produce the finished components in quantity. The largest pattern is the floor of the car, made of synthetic high density board, which takes two weeks to machine before it is ready to perform its duty as the mould for the approximately 90 carbon fibre floors the team will need for the 8 to 10 chassis that will be used during a season. Less exotic timbers are used to make the gearbox mould from which metal sand castings are made, though because of its complexity the gearbox pattern requires six weeks to manufacture.

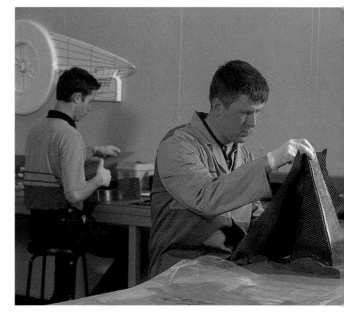

composites shop

One of the most labour intensive areas in the factory is the Composites Shop, managed by Dave Hawke, where some 3500 different components (over 70 per cent of the car) are produced, many of them from carbon fibre which is used for the basic monocoque, body panels, wings, steering wheel, even suspension components. The 34 people in Composites, who work in shifts, day and night, are all carbon fibre enthusiasts and enjoy explaining its wonderful properties and its surprisingly elemental content. In fact, a primitive form of carbon fibre existed in ancient Egypt. Horse hair was used to manufacture bricks that were then heated so that the hair formed carbon strands, which provided the extra strength that enabled many monumental Egyptian edifices to stand the test of time.

Composite technicians Paul Whitbread and Steve Roake. The Composites Shop produces some 3500 different components – over 70 per cent of the car.

The factory floor. The brightly lit, spotlessly clean, purposeful labyrinth where the cars are built.

Modern carbon fibre is produced by heating and stretching acrylic fibres (similar to artificial wool), first in air and then in argon, a nitrogen-enriched atmosphere. This process aligns the carbon atoms to give the qualities of stiffness and lightness that are so much desired in a F1 chassis. The individual fibres are woven into a fabric that is impregnated with an epoxy resin, then frozen to prevent pre-curing and shipped in that state by the manufacturer, to McLaren where it is stored in freezers.

The Composites technicians cut, trim and weave the pliable sheets of carbon fibre over the moulds in staggered layers. As many as 10 layers are sandwiched with aluminium honeycomb to form the car's nose cone. After this 'laying up' procedure the component in its mould is consolidated in a vacuum bag, placed in a huge, computer-controlled oven called an autoclave and heated at 120 degrees centigrade for up to four hours. The end result is a component that is five times lighter than steel but twice as strong, so that a complete carbon fibre chassis weighs about 40kg.

Dave Johnson in the Machine Shop, where aluminium, titanium, tungsten and steel components are produced with a design accuracy that falls within 0.0004mm.

Not only items destined for the cars come out of Composites. One recent project was to produce 30 new helmets for the Race Team pit crew to use in 1998. Designed by a team led by Andy Blackmore, McLaren's product designer, and based on an evolution of the modified Carrera ski helmets used previously, the stylish new black helmets made from carbon fibre are 13 per cent lighter, despite having 33 per cent greater surface area to improve soundproofing protection and the positioning of the Kenwood intercom systems. To prevent fuel from splashing into the eyes of the pit crew, the helmet goggles were fitted with an oversize silver lens, deliberately designed to achieve a fighter pilot effect. Including baking in the autoclave and fitting the interior padding, each helmet took about 11 hours to manufacture. They were then sent to the Paint Shop where, over three days, the McLaren livery was applied, including the nicknames of the members of the pit crew. The whole process to produce 30 helmets took three months.

machine shop

Another major manufacturing centre in the factory is the Machine Shop, where Manager Nick Lloyd's group consists of about 25 people who work in shifts (on average about 50 hours per week, per person, per year) to produce most of the components not made from carbon fibre. These include all the running gear for the car – everything from 3 millimetre diameter washers, to suspension bell cranks and wishbone bearings, to all the gears (59 pairs of gears) in the gearbox. With machinery (valued at £8 million) that is 80 per cent computer controlled, the Machine Shop produces components (with a design accuracy that falls within 0.0004mm) from four main types of metal: aluminium, titanium, tungsten and steel.

fabrication shop

The Fabrication Shop, with a workforce of eight highly skilled artisans managed by Pete Burns, is responsible for hand crafting over 70 items on the car. These include the brake and accelerator pedals (individually designed and hand built to suit each driver), suspension uprights (each one of which takes 40 hours to complete in a process that involves pattern cutting, bending, welding and assembly), water radiators, oil coolers, whatever other suspension components not made from carbon fibre, and the exhaust systems, over 50 of which each season are bent and shaped from Iconel steel like pieces of complex sculpture.

right: **Bob Smith welding a suspension upright in the Fabrication Shop, where a skilled workforce handcrafts over 70 items on the car.**

below: **Gary Harrison working on an exhaust system, over 50 of which each season are bent and shaped like pieces of complex sculpture.**

electronics

Speaking of complexity, the electronic systems on the car that link together more than 100 sensors, actuators and control units, require a wiring 'harness' that is approximately 1000 metres long. The electronic heart of the car is found in a small black box that sits in front of the engine. This is the TAG 2000 Electronic Management System, an integrated engine, chassis control and data acquisition system that controls the Mercedes engine, the gearbox, throttle, clutch, differential – everything that is electronic on the car. The TAG 2000 unit also logs everything that is under electronic control on the car (24 megabytes of data, equivalent to the amount of information in two London telephone directories) concerning the engine and chassis from the sensors on the car and transfers it back to the pits from the track at a rate of 4 million bits per second. A further 4Mbytes of detailed information is sent to the pits in concentrated bursts each time the car passes by.

Trevor Lawes, gearbox specialist, also travels with the Race Team. The six-speed gearbox is capable of executing shifts within 20 to 40 milliseconds.

This electronic marvel is made by McLaren International's associate company TAG Electronic Systems. TES, set up in 1989 and now employing 120 people, is run by Chief Executive Officer Dr Udo Zucker, an award-winning physicist. Besides supplying the TES 2000 unit to the McLaren team, and also in 1998 to the Jordan, Prost and Arrows teams, TES sells its products to over 80 customers in the automotive industry, including automobile manufacturers Mercedes–Benz, Peugeot, BMW, Porsche and Toyota.

gearbox

In the factory's Gearbox Department, Manager Neil Trundle and his seven men are responsible for the six-speed, semi-automatic, computer-controlled, magnesium-encased unit that is designed and built in-house. Capable of executing shifts in the blink of an eye – from 20 to 40 milliseconds – each gearbox has up to 59 gear ratios available and the team takes an average of six gearboxes to each race.

The actual gears, the six pairs of cogs that transfer the power from the Mercedes engine, are manufactured from aircraft quality steel (produced under vacuum and melted twice to drive out impurities) and cut by a specialized Charmilles Technologies Robofil EDM wire-cutting machine, installed in the factory in 1995.

Neil, one of the longest serving McLaren employees, and other veterans such as his foreman Colin Patrick, a McLaren man for 20 years, use their lengthy experience to produce gearboxes – from 16 to 20 each year – that in several recent seasons achieved nearly 100 per cent reliability.

'Back in the old days,' Neil recalls, 'in the Lauda/Prost era, we only ran with five gearboxes and had only one guy looking after them. But they were a lot simpler then and the gearbox side has expanded vastly over the years. Here, we do preparation, initial box build, rebuilds, maintenance, development and experimental work. It's quite time consuming but that's what you need for reliability.'

quality control

The continual emphasis on reliability means every component is subjected to rigorous quality control measures. A computer-based co-ordinate measuring machine measures components three dimensionally, by means of a moving electronic probe, to check that the finished product measures up to its design specification. Metal components are carefully inspected following surface, crack testing and heat treatment procedures. Since each component is designed to function optimally for a specific period of time (in some cases limited to the two hours of a race), the system of 'lifing' (whereby the date each component is manufactured is recorded) ensures a component is not used beyond its 'sell by' date.

When the components are assembled into a finished car they must also undergo rigorous crash tests – including front, rear and side impact tests – to conform to the stringent F1 safety regulations. However, before that happens every single component is subjected to a battery of tests in the factory.

materials

Someone who specializes in component testing is Paul Cox, team leader in the Materials Department. Paul was formerly a scientific officer with the Royal Aircraft Establishment (now the Defence Research Agency), an appropriate background for his job at McLaren, which requires him to confirm that components are produced to aircraft standards. 'We are the last link in the chain. The possibility of a component failing has to be eliminated before it gets near the car. It's a job where nothing can be taken for granted. The risks are simply too high,' Paul says of his discipline. He also notes his area of research and development is sometimes called 'Wreck and Destroy' and that others in the factory claim 'We make it, Paul breaks it'.

"They are there to impress, but not so much the visitors as the people working here. They never see the cars complete and they can lose sight of why they are working so hard. Each of the cars has the engine, gearbox and suspension it had when it crossed the finish line. These cars have pedigree."
Ron Dennis
(on the cars in reception)

In most cases, components are first taken to their design limits, then as far beyond them as they will go. To test the rear pushrods in the suspension system, Paul and his people subject them to forces equivalent to supporting the weight of two heavy road cars from them. A load of 8 tons is used to test the strength of the chassis roll hoop. Among the purpose-built component testing machines are two Instron mechanical frames, one static (to test strength and stiffness) and the other dynamic (to recreate the stresses and strains components are subjected to on individual Grand Prix circuits). Using the latter, suspension pushrods and wishbones can be put through 1000 race laps, equivalent to a full season, in under 24 hours. Similarly, the Instron 30 ton test rig – the 'four poster' – is used to test the complete car in simulated race conditions. A typical three-day test session on the four poster will produce 500 sheets of data.

Says Paul Cox: 'There is a new challenge every day and as long as the only things that go wrong do so within these four walls, I know we're doing our job right.'

paint shop

In many cases the work of the skilled personnel in the factory combines both art and technology. Certainly, this is so in the Paint Shop, where Manager George Langhorn and his six talented airbrush artists are responsible for applying to the bodywork the distinctive visual identity that makes the gleaming West McLaren Mercedes cars among the most admired in the racing world. The Paint Shop also transfers the McLaren image onto every piece of the team's equipment that goes to the races – from the trucks, to the fuel rigs, the generators and the wall panels in the garage.

'The new car is more of a work of art than it used to be,' George explains, 'with a series of amorphous lines and graphite grey areas to be separately airbrushed, before a final lacquer and polish. The new colour scheme features a number of coats: Mercedes Brilliant Silver, intermediate graphite greys for the amorphous lines, a base coat white and a day-glo red on the nose.

'A great deal of precision is also necessary to ensure perfect inter-changeability. For example, we send six noses to each race and every one must be capable of matching an individual chassis perfectly. To help achieve 100 per cent compatibility a fully painted mock-up chassis is retained in the Paint Shop at all times. Every two or three races each chassis will be stripped down to its primer coat and completely re-painted.'

George, who has been with McLaren for many years, and who once worked as a tyre man with the Race Team, is known in the factory as 'Teardrop'. According to George, his nickname was earned from two separate incidents in the distant past when blemishes marred his usual state of painterly perfection. Once, two aluminium chassis he sprayed developed 'a little run from almost every rivet. Then, in 1976, the first McLaren IndyCar to race in orange trim had a huge run from one end to the other. It went on to win the Indianapolis 500, but it seems some people remember it for my handiwork as opposed to what the car achieved.'

George's handiwork, as applied to decorating helmets, has always been appreciated by McLaren's drivers. Among those sporting helmets customized by Teardrop were John Watson, Niki Lauda, Alain Prost and the late Ayrton Senna. The tradition is continued these days, with both Mika Hakkinen and David Coulthard using helmets styled by Teardrop. McLaren's technical and commercial partners also rely on George's expert eye, since he (along with Ron Dennis and people from the team's graphics department) is entrusted with applying their decals in precisely predetermined positions on the painted bodywork

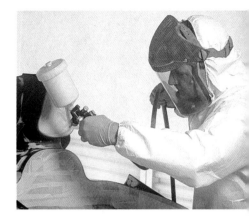

top: **George Langhorn (along with his talented airbrush artists) apply the team's distinctive visual identity to every piece of equipment.**

bottom: **In the Paint Shop, Mike Renney and Gary Beaumont transform chassis sections into gleaming examples of their handiwork.**

1

2

assembly

The work in the Paint Shop is one of the final stages in the process of assembling the components into a finished car. After the carbon fibre chassis has been cured in the autoclave and painted it is moved into the car build area for final assembly. The first installation is the fuel cell (constructed of two layers of Nitrile-Buta-dien Rubber), which is positioned directly behind the driver's seat. Then the Mercedes engine (shipped to the factory from Ilmor Engineering) is put on for the first time. Over the next few weeks a constant stream of parts are added as they filter through from the various departments in the factory.

Once the chassis floor, bodywork, nose cone, rear wing, exhaust system, and front and rear suspensions are in place – which takes about two weeks – a recognizable car has taken shape. A week later, when the water and oil systems are added and the wiring harness installation is completed, the car is mechanically almost finished and

Once all the components have been assembled, the deafening howl of the V10 engine announces the birth of a brand new West McLaren Merecedes F1 car.

emerges from the sub-assembly area as a rolling chassis. A couple of days later, after all systems have been checked and double-checked, the Mercedes–Benz V10 is fired up for the first time, its deafening howl announcing the birth of a brand new West McLaren Mercedes car.

spares

A list of all the components that make up a car runs to nearly 40 pieces of paper. The man who knows this master list intimately is Chris 'Robbo' Robson, the spares co-ordinator. Robbo's list, which everyone calls 'The Bible', includes everything from head restraints to hydraulic bleed nipples, O-ring seals,

mirror lenses, steering arms, brake ducts, wishbones and brake banjo washers. When the Race (or Test) Team leaves the factory Robbo and his men send with it enough spare components – which are listed on an abridged version of The Bible, running to 29 pages – to cover most contingencies. Even then, Robbo admits, 'There is always something that needs to be taken to an event at the last minute and it's very rare that anyone going out after the main group isn't given some sort of component to take with them.

Spares co-ordinator Chris Robson (right, with Mike Negline) has a list of all the components of the car which runs to nearly 40 sheets of paper.

'Everything we make in the factory has a drawing and a part number, and a serial number that is engraved on that part. For every section of the car there is an official list of all the parts that go together to make it. It's not just the car, but the different specifications of wings and suspension, all the variations and options, and all the spares and equipment to back it up when you go racing or testing. We keep track of every part so that we can see where it was used, when it was used, when it was crack-checked, proof-checked and so on. We put a life on these items, so we know when it shouldn't be used any more. The people on the Race Team and the Test Team keep us informed of any problems with components, as well as their mileage and performance record. When we have any shortages I chase Production and make sure new components are built.'

When the components leave the factory Robbo admits to momentary feelings of wanderlust, for he spent about 20 years on the road himself. He joined McLaren in 1973, then went to Brabham for a while, before returning to McLaren in 1987, as chief truckie on the Race Team.

'It was a bit of a culture shock when the opportunity to take on the Spares job came up. I struggled for a while to come to terms with not travelling. At first, I hated staying behind here at the factory. But what you don't miss are the long hours on the road, the extended hours at the airport and the 13-hour flights to the "flyaway" races, getting back at one o'clock in the morning after a race weekend, never having a day off to mow the lawn or things like that. What you do miss is the fantastic atmosphere that goes with a race. But I'm not complaining. This is a good job. I've really got into it now and it's great to still be closely involved and play your part with the guys who go racing.'

Robbo's Spares Department is listed as part of the Race Team and he still gets to fraternize with those who do the travelling, since the Race and Test Teams are based at the factory. Their presence is a reminder to all who stay behind that their contribution, no matter how far removed from the Grand Prix circuits, is vital to keeping the McLaren show on the road. Also inspirational for the Home Team are such former 'racers' as Peter Hennessy, whose electricians, painters and cleaners in the Factory Services department work day and night shifts in support of the team effort.

clothing
In many ways, the highly disciplined, ultra-functional McLaren team resembles an army, an effect that is heightened by the uniforms worn by the employees. Until recently only those who travelled to the circuits were issued with team gear, but now those who work on the factory floor are similarly attired.

The team's apparel is supplied by Hugo Boss AG, a leading menswear fashion house and a commercial partner of McLaren since 1984. The clothing is produced in Germany and sent to the factory where it is kept in the Clothing Store. The store is as densely packed with garments as a large retail emporium, a high fashion one at that since the clothing is designed by Mauro Taliano, one of the main sportswear designers for Hugo Boss. The store holds up to four complete sets of outfits for everyone who requires some sort of team uniform.

In the factory the workforce wardrobe – called the 'Base Kit' – consists of grey smocks, black polo-neck sweaters, grey striped shirts (for supervisors and department heads), two shades of grey polo shirts, grey sweatshirts in two styles (one traditional and one modern), black trousers and black shoes.

Bobby Barratt in the Clothing Store, where the drivers' uniforms and the wardrobes of the Home and Race Teams are kept.

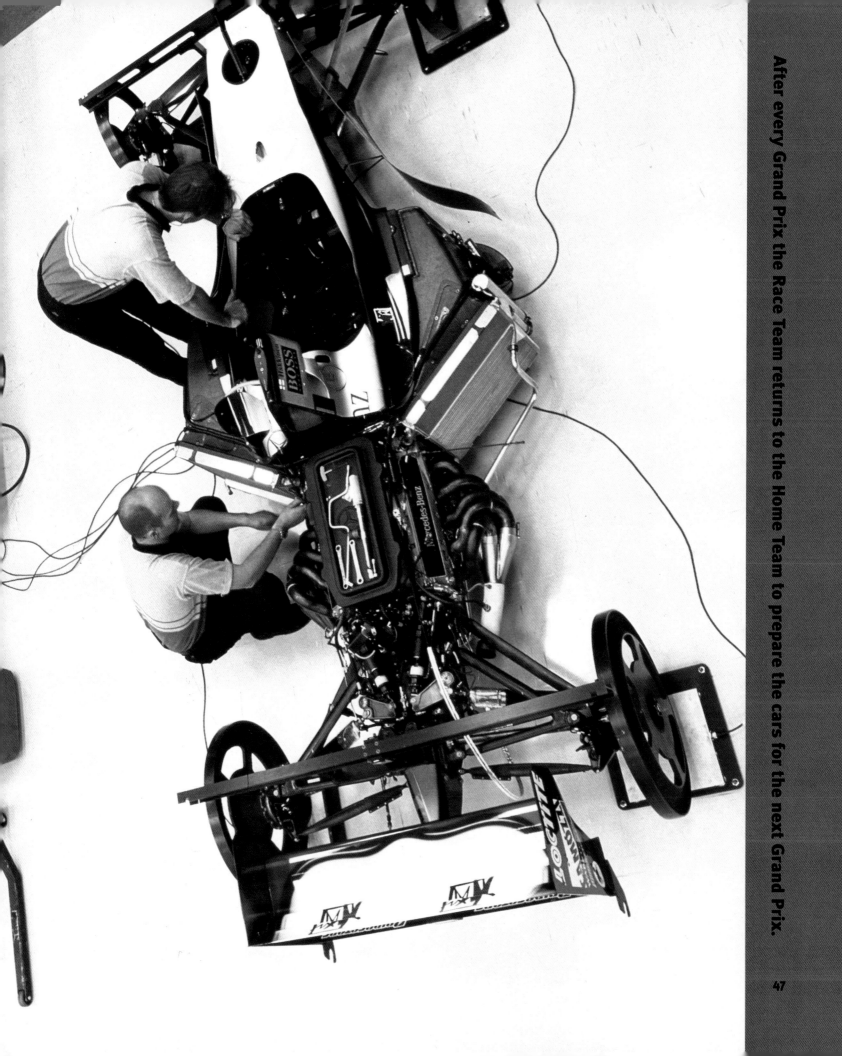

For travelling, each member of the team is issued with a brown corduroy blazer, a white and blue checked shirt, charcoal grey trousers, brown belt and brown suede shoes. For work at the circuits the personnel have black shoes, four pairs of black socks, four pairs of black trousers, four pairs of black shorts, four team shirts (with their names embroidered on the pockets), two grey jumpers, one grey jacket, one waterproof reflective jacket, one reflective body warmer, one reflective padded jacket, one reflective belt and one watch. There are three separate sets of these garments designed to suit the advertising emphasis in different countries. Every garment is made to measure so that it fits each person perfectly. Over the race weekend they might change costume several times but everyone must be dressed exactly the same all the time. After each race every garment is cleaned and pressed, and after every fourth race some of the clothing is replaced.

Ryan Lewis, who now looks after merchandising with TAG McLaren Marketing Services, formerly worked in the Clothing Store as the clothing co-ordinator. 'We order a complete new range of clothing for the start of every season, which involves not only clothing McLaren personnel but also our partners as far afield as Germany, Italy and Japan, for a total of about 150 people. It takes some organizing and it goes beyond just matching everyone's size. When a new partner is taken on board almost everything has to be changed and updated to include their logos.'

Ryan notes that the fastidiousness of those who wear the clothing extends throughout the team. 'It's surprising how fussy everyone is about their clothes. When it comes to picking up their clean kit, suddenly they want their trousers turned up an extra half inch in the back and everything has to look just so. When they come back from a race you've only got about four days to get everything cleaned, pressed, mended, altered and ready to go again. We've got a lady here in Woking whose full-time job, night and day, is sewing, mending and making alterations. Monogramming everybody's names on the clothing is also a huge task. For the shirts you have to take off the pockets to get them monogrammed, for 150 people, then sew them back on again. It's a tremendous amount of work, but it's the way McLaren does things. It's all about image and at McLaren we believe it's got to be 100 per cent perfect at all times.'

marketing

Most of the work relating to the McLaren image is handled by TAG McLaren Marketing Services, a division of the company that enjoys a reputation for being the most sophisticated and successful marketing organization in motorsport. McLaren International has a 'Vision statement: To compete in and win every Formula 1 race'. The team's marketing wing is similarly single-minded and dedicated to the philosophy outlined in the TAG McLaren corporate overview. 'The determination to succeed and constantly strive for excellence has made McLaren International a world class competitor in the most visually competitive of market places. It is this constant search for excellence and success that allows McLaren International to gain maximum mileage from Formula 1 in terms of commercial exposure.'

"I'm a very competitive person. I want to win in business and I want to win on the track. But we've always encouraged our partners to have a long-term relationship. Interestingly, when we weren't winning, from 1994 to 1996, we increased the corporate investment in the company."

Ekrem Sami

TAG McLaren Marketing Services, which was formed in 1987 to serve the marketing requirements of McLaren International, now has 30 employees. There are five departments within TMMS: Partner Management (helping team investors get the maximum marketing benefit from their involvement), Client Services (providing hospitality at the races and promotional opportunities for partners and guests), Creative (responsible for the design and production of everything to do with the McLaren image), Business Development (finding new partners) and Communications (handling media relations and the image of the company).

The first name on the list of TAG McLaren Marketing Services personnel is Ekrem Sami, now managing director of TMMS and before that a pioneer in the field of marketing as it relates to racing. While still at college, where he was studying Business Administration, Ekrem met Ron Dennis who invited him to travel around Europe with the Project Four F2 team for the 1977 season. At first Ekrem was the team gofer, doing everything from sweeping the floors to polishing the cars. When he finished college he began working full time with Ron, looking after the books, wages and purchasing and becoming increasingly involved in developing the business side of the operation. By the time McLaren International was formed, in 1980, Ron and Ekrem had devised a

Ekrem Sami, managing director of TAG McLaren Marketing Services, is a pioneer in the field of marketing as it relates to racing.

strategy of selling the team, acquiring new partners and sponsors and building long-term relationships with major corporations.

Over the years few teams have been as successful as McLaren when it comes to developing the business side of what is undoubtedly the most expensive sport in the world. This is Ekrem Sami's particular area of expertise and he describes his main focus as 'extending the business relationships we have with existing partners, introducing new companies into partnership with McLaren and looking to enhance the McLaren brand.

Stewart Goodwin, Russell Harvey, Diana Kay, Alan Firman and Greg Brogan of TMMS Graphics Department, which is also responsible for creating the team's brand.

'From a business development perspective, the kind of goal we set ourselves is to generate significantly more revenue in the company than any other team but at the same time assemble a world class group of complimentary partners. We think we've got a premium product and we charge a premium price for it. But to retain that there's got to be the delivery, both on and off the track. At the end of the day, a lot of what you are selling is yourself, and to do that you've got to believe in the product you're selling. I have complete belief and faith in this organization, and that McLaren can deliver.

'From the outside, McLaren is sometimes perceived as cold, perhaps because we're seen as very calculating, very focused, with a real commitment to winning. Underneath the surface we're actually quite a warm and friendly organization. There's a good feeling of family. I think we have a very high level of integrity, which is very important in terms of what we are selling. McLaren has a very strong corporate culture that emanates down from Ron because, at the end of the day, the company is a reflection of his values, first and foremost. In a nutshell, it is a quest for continuous improvement toward perfection, to be the best in everything we do.'

In their quest for perfection Ekrem and his TMMS colleagues are detail conscious in the extreme. The receptionists in the lobby at headquarters are chosen for their warm personalities and pleasant telephone manner. When partners or prospective partners come to visit McLaren their corporate colours are reflected in vases full of fresh flowers, and in the executive dining room the McLaren 'M' logo is sculpted in the pats of butter on the table.

As Ekrem says: 'We constantly think about that kind of attention to detail and if we miss something Ron is sure to pick it up. A while ago a vase in reception was changed from opaque to clear glass. Ron came into reception and noticed you could see the water in the vase. He picked up the fact that by two or three in the afternoon that water would be murky and slimy, so the vase had to be changed. The level of attention to detail that guy has is quite amazing, and we try and instil that value into everybody and reflect it throughout the company, from the moment you walk in the front door.'

Peter Stayner describes when he first walked in the McLaren door in 1989: 'What came across immediately was the high level of presentation – the reception area, the trophies, the cars, the whole factory – the immaculateness of everything, the precision, the detail. It had an aura. There was a feeling of excitement, of anticipation, that this was McLaren, where the Grand Prix team lives, where the cars are born. When you walked inside that building you knew you were somewhere very special.'

Ekrem Sami (here with Prince Albert of Monaco) and the TMMS personnel develop new business and provide management services for partners and clients.

As head of Partner Management at TMMS, it is part of Peter Stayner's job to ensure his clients are similarly moved when they visit McLaren, a task he performs with unforced enthusiasm, since he still feels the same way. ('It really is a privileged place to visit, and to work, as Ron keeps reminding us!') Before he joined McLaren Peter applied his appreciation of motorsport, which was inherited from his father ('a great motoring man'), to the workaday world by becoming a manager of several race circuits (including Brands Hatch). He was also involved on the organizational and marketing side with the RAC Motorsport Association in London.

Nowadays, Peter's duties at TMMS still take him to the races, where he is in charge of looking after the team's corporate guests. 'Part of our job is to make sure our guests have a good time. We have to make sure they've got the proper passes, show them around the pits, let them talk to the drivers and generally keep the guests comfortable throughout the weekend. We have to keep them interested and entertained and show them they're spending their money wisely, so they go away with a very good feeling about Formula 1 and about their company being involved in it with us.'

Peter notes that when it comes to appreciating the marketing side of McLaren some people take the old-fashioned view: 'They think that all we're doing is drinking champagne all day and showing glamorous women around the pits. Sometimes the perception is that marketing is just an add-on, a bolt-on bit. But that quickly changes when they see instances where marketing hasn't worked and F1 teams don't make it, because their funding dries up. It's all very much a part of racing now and everybody in marketing feels very close to the team.

'Win or lose, we go through all the emotions with them, from elation to disappointment. We share the emotion, throughout the whole team. And that's a big thing with McLaren. There is a family feeling and we try to make our partners feel like part of the family. We look after them very well and, as Ekrem keeps telling me, we spend more on partner management than anybody else. But it's the way we do things at McLaren. It's all part of the image.'

One of those most responsible for projecting McLaren's image is Anna Guerrier, head of Media Communications. At the races, where her duties include dealing with the vast contingent of international media representatives, Anna is one of the most public faces of the team on the world's stage, a role for which her multifarious background was excellent preparation. She studied English, art and history, then went to drama school and got her Equity card. Anna did some acting (musical theatre was her preference), then began working as a stage manager for a company producing shows in London's West End theatres. Introduced to motorsport by her husband, who does some racing and rallying, she started writing freelance race reports, and also worked as a BBC radio reporter and a television presenter on shows that included motorsport. In 1995, when she applied for a position with TMMS, her past experience and her sparkling personality made her ideally suited for getting McLaren's message across to the public.

'It was a bit scary,' Anna remembers, 'having to go through about five interviews to get the job. The standards here are so high and it seemed intimidating. But it was worth it and I'm very happy doing this work. We have a really good group of people and the guys on the team are such fun. The human side is what makes this the team it is and that makes it easier to communicate what we stand for. We try to communicate quality, the leading edge of technology, the experience and expertise of the workforce, and our exceptionally high standards, higher than you would find in most industries, let alone Formula 1 racing.'

Central to communicating McLaren's image is the 'colouration' of the corporate identity that gives the team its visual personality. In 1997, after 23 years of being red and white (the colours of major partner Marlboro), the McLaren corporate colours were changed to variations on a silver-grey theme with red highlights. The colours were chosen to merge the identities of the team's major partners – including new partner West, as well as the historic 'Silver Arrows' motif of engine supplier Mercedes – into the McLaren 'brand'.

Anna Guerrier, Head of Media Communications, deals with the large contingent of international media representatives at the races.

the image

To effect the change of identity, proposals were invited from six design firms – three from the UK and three from Germany – to compete with a baseline concept created by the graphic designers in the TMMS Creative Department, which is headed by Andy Mackenzie. A former illustrator who had his own production company before joining McLaren in 1990, Andy says: 'Our goal is to reflect the image of a professional business, not a razzmatazz race team. We are a high technology, high profile, highly efficient business and our job is to portray that visually.

'One of the main philosophies behind the new design was to develop a brand identity for McLaren. Previously, and it's still that way with other teams, anybody associated with the team just stuck their identity on the cars and uniforms and you had a mish-mash of confusing graphics and colours. It's much better to have one package, where the partners buy the right to put their names on the McLaren brand. So, when the opportunity came to claim back our identity we grabbed it with both hands.'

Among the creative hands in Andy Mackenzie's department is Design Manager Diana Kay, who has a degree in Graphics from the London College of Printing, and who has been with TMMS for eight years. Diana, together with Andy, Ron Dennis and several others, was part of an imaging strategy group that went through a lengthy process of changing the McLaren image.

'We started by analysing the way the company was perceived,' Diana recalls. 'It was seen to be predatory, always hungry for victory and chasing after it in every race. We wanted to convey that feeling of aggression, as well as elements of efficiency and precision. It also had to be dynamic and stylish. We like to keep things clean and not have a lot of clutter. Our initial brief was that we wanted a car with no hard definition of straight lines, the way conventional racing cars are done. We wanted to define colour in transition and to keep it clean, instead of having a mixture of different colours fighting against each other.

Andy Mackenzie's goal as head of the TMMS Creative Department is to reflect the image of a high technology, high profile, highly efficient business.

"The real highlight was the 'Wow' factor when the car was first shown to the public before the start of the season".

'What evolved from our thinking was what we now refer to as the "amorphous" design, where graphite silver oval shapes blend into each other, with black to give it body and white to soften it up a bit, and with rocket red highlights, like on the nose of the car, to give it aggression. We carried that aggressive theme into the new McLaren logo, which is the rocket red, amorphous tick – like a shark's fin.

'After we finished the concepts, we then applied them to model cars and kept refining the design all the time until we applied it to a full-scale car. Once it was sprayed up full size, we were pretty sure it worked. The real highlight was the "Wow" factor when the car was first shown to the public, at Alexandra Palace before the start of the 1997 season. There were thousands of people and when the car was unveiled there was this huge audible gasp. And it was at that moment when I thought, "Oh yes, it's right. It worked!" It was so thrilling – wonderfully pleasing for all of us who were deeply involved with it. We'd been living it night and day for such a long time.'

catering

If an army marches on its stomach then the McLaren team is particularly well-nourished to go the distance, though it doesn't have to travel far to receive its sustenance. At headquarters there are two main eating areas – The Restaurant (which has two chefs) and The Bistro (where the chef is a Cypriot who once owned his own restaurant) – as well as a visitors' dining room. Nearby, there are three smaller satellite catering units to serve the employees at McLaren Cars, TAG Electronics and TAG McLaren Marketing Services. The man in charge of feeding the troops is Michael Edgecombe, the catering manager.

Michael, whose background included hotel and industrial catering, has been with McLaren for five years and, though very much a team man, he refers to those he feeds as his 'customers', and to serve them he has a philosophy of equal treatment. 'If I'm serving a visiting VIP, or if I'm serving someone who's working on the shop floor, they're equally important to me. They're still our customers and to be a success you need to serve good food by polite people in a nice atmosphere.'

If an army marches on its stomach then the McLaren team is particularly well-nourished to go the distance... At headquarters there are two main eating areas as well as a visitors' dining room.

This being McLaren, Michael and his catering crew put a great deal of effort into presentation. 'Take the table settings, everything has to be perfect. When we lay out the cutlery, the knives have to be perfectly straight and all the utensils placed just so. We place the food on the plates in a decorative way, not over the top, or "frilly" as Ron would say. Ron likes everything to be very clean, very simple, but very well-presented, down to the last detail.'

Those details include accommodating the particular tastes of visitors, and while Michael serves everything from 'meat and two veg' to 'cuisine nouvelle' on a daily basis, the catering effort is stepped up a notch when special guests arrive.

'These are often people accustomed to eating at the best restaurants around the world, so we have to be able to match that level of cuisine. And if they are vegetarians or eat certain foods for religious or medical reasons, we feed them accordingly. If we have what I call a normal type group of visitors we would serve them a buffet, with a choice of three hot main courses, two meat and one vegetarian choice, a choice of several salads, a choice of three desserts, and coffee. It's quite an informal atmosphere, although it looks quite stunning when they arrive.

'I always get flowers and ribbons to match the corporate colours of a company that might be visiting. We start at the front door and tie everything together, from when they walk into reception and the trophy room, right the way through to the dining room. We think of every little detail. It's what we're known for. It's part of McLaren.

'You know, when I first came here I didn't actually know much about Formula 1 and I had to do some research about who was driving for us and where we were in the championships. Now, it's amazing, because you are part of it and you are sucked into this whirlwind of activity. I'm very lucky because I get to know everybody on the team – the drivers, the partners, everybody involved. They all come in here to eat and whatever is happening at the races you can pick everything up from the mood of your customers.

'Absolutely the worst time for us was after Ayrton Senna was killed, in 1994. He wasn't driving for us then, but we all remembered him and after it happened the atmosphere in here was incredibly low. It was just a great cloud of gloom that descended over everything and everybody was so sad. It took a long time to get over that. On the other hand, when the team does well, you get the opposite emotion and you can feel the elation. No matter what happens, it affects the overall mood and you can feel it here. On a race weekend we have the television on in the restaurants and on a Monday we show the race on video. People just sit there. They forget about what's on their plates. They're only interested in watching how the team is doing.'

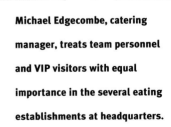

Michael Edgecombe, catering manager, treats team personnel and VIP visitors with equal importance in the several eating establishments at headquarters.

the originals

"Something like this has a bit of everybody in McLaren in it, going back to when Bruce won that first Grand Prix, and even before then."

RON DENNIS
(accepting an award given to McLaren for becoming the most successful F1 team, 1993)

McLaren memories

During tea breaks at the Woking factory it is the custom of some of the veteran employees to sit around the same table and reminisce about the early days of the team. It is said that to qualify for a seat at the table one must be able to tell tall tales of McLaren's races at Watkins Glen, the American circuit that last held a Grand Prix in 1980. In these gatherings to relive McLaren memories the conversations are lively and punctuated by lots of laughter. And while those in conversation are often called 'The Wrinklies', the old-timers tend to look younger than their years, as if their mutual passion for racing, for McLaren, is like a fountain of youth.

"The good thing about this organization is that, despite achieving great success, we've never become complacent."

Nowadays, the likes of George Langhorn, Peter Hodgman, Peter Hennessy and Chris Robson concentrate their expertise on running their departments in the factory. But in their previous labours they had a hand in laying the very foundations of the team that McLaren eventually became. Other charter members of The Wrinklies are Ian Barnard, head of Transport, Gary Walker, an assembly supervisor, and Barry Ultahan and Ian Dyer of the Test Team. Their continuing presence in the team helps to provide valuable continuity in the complex organization McLaren has become. And the collective team spirit of the veterans, based on many years of loyal service, is a vital component in maintaining morale in what is still a very close-knit workforce.

'Barnie' Barnard, head of Transport, is a charter member of The Wrinklies.

None of The Wrinklies has been around longer than Ray 'Tex' Rowe, who joined McLaren virtually as it came into existence. Ray began working as a mechanic for the Cooper F1 team in 1961. When Bruce McLaren left Cooper to set up his own team, Ray followed. Then 29 years old, Ray remembers the date well. It was 1 April 1965, and since then he has worked on just about every car McLaren has produced.

These days Ray, nicknamed Tex for his keen interest in western movies, is a stalwart in the Sub-Assembly team at Woking. In his spare time he builds component cars for himself and his son, with a high degree of workmanship that has won the Rowe-built vehicles prizes in competition.

Ray loves the excitement of racing competition, though he notes that the intensity is diluted somewhat now because, 'in the old days we all pitched in and did a bit of everything. With specialization you haven't got the sense of total participation we used to have. We're split up and work in groups, but at the end of the day it's good to see the whole thing turn out well and know that you've been a part of it. When things don't go so well you've got to keep your head down and get on with it. The good thing about this organization is that, despite achieving great success, we've never become complacent. That's the way it's been from the beginning. The other thing is that so much of what we do now is controlled by computers. But at the end of the day it's not just the computers. It doesn't come from them. It still comes from the people.'

'Robbo' Robson started in 1973 and travelled with the Race Team for many years.

According to Ray, the most important person in the team has always been its leader, a tradition that began with its founder. 'Bruce was a likeable, modest man. He was very much a "doer" and led us by example. When he wasn't racing or testing he could always be found in the factory pushing things along. When Bruce was killed, in 1970, we desperately needed someone inspirational to maintain the momentum. We were lucky Ron Dennis came along to do that. And it still gives everybody a big boost when he comes around the factory to chat.'

The chat of The Wrinklies is peppered with flashbacks into the team's origins. Particularly well-placed to provide insights into how Bruce McLaren Racing Limited became the organization it is today is Neil Trundle. Nicknamed 'Tinker' for his habit of busily tinkering away at whatever task is at hand, Neil's duties these days are confined mainly to the Gearbox department he manages, though with his long memory he could easily qualify as the team's official historian.

'Teardrop' Langhorn, veteran team man and story-teller *par excellence.*

Neil started his working life as an apprentice with the Ford Motor Company, where he became involved in weekend club racing activities with some of his workmates and 'got the bug'. In 1968 he joined Jack Brabham's team, working as a mechanic in both F1 and IndyCar racing. In those days the Brabham workforce included people like Peter Hennessy, now head of Factory Services at McLaren, and also Ron Dennis, who became Brabham's chief mechanic in 1970.

right: **In the old days the working conditions and the equipment were all quite primitive compared to the way things are now.**

'We were eight mechanics who ran the whole Formula 1 team,' Neil recalls. 'We built the cars in the winter and went racing in the summer, travelling together in the truck with the cars in the back. No airplanes in those days. We would drive 24 hours non-stop to places like Monza, taking shifts at the wheel, some guys sleeping in the cab or in the back on the hammock Ron strung up between the work benches. We were a really close bunch, working together, eating together, socializing together.'

It was all quite primitive compared to the way McLaren works now, but even in those early days Neil notes how Brabham differed from other teams, and how the person largely responsible for it was the chief mechanic.

'Ron was the ringleader, passionate about his racing and the one that always fired up the enthusiasm in the rest of us. He was a very, very good race mechanic and always absolutely meticulous about preparation. In 1970 Jack Brabham's cars were the best looking in the pit lane, the shiniest, the cleanest, the best-prepared. It was the same way back at the factory. I remember Ron Tauranac (designer of the Brabham cars) went away on a week's holiday and Ron Dennis instigated painting the whole workshop – did most of it himself. We used to call him a bit of an old woman, but anything to do with cleanliness and preparation, he instigated it and you couldn't deny that it paid off. And Ron was very ambitious, a go-getter, always has been.'

The collective team spirit of the veterans, based on many years of loyal service, is a vital component in maintaining morale in what is still a very close-knit workforce.

At the end of 1970, Ron persuaded Neil that they should strike out on their own with a Formula 2 team. They called themselves Rondel Racing and Ron brought in a financial partner (Tony Vlassopolus, a shipping magnate) to underwrite the initial funding. Using borrowed cars (from Ron Tauranac who continued running Brabham after Jack retired at the end of 1970) and engines (from Bernie Ecclestone, who bought Brabham and went on effectively to run F1 racing itself), and basing themselves in a workshop in Woking (loaned by its owner Maurice Gomm) Dennis and Trundle went F2 racing.

'We begged, borrowed and scrounged,' Neil remembers. 'We lived with Ron's parents. They kept us and fed us for a year to help get the thing going. That was in 1971, and we were going good, until Ron had his massive car crash in the summer of '72. We were exhausted, doing nearly everything ourselves. We had worked all night to get the cars ready for a race at Crystal Palace, repainting them to make them look like a million dollars – as only Ron knew how to do. Coming back from the race I was driving the truck and he was in his Jaguar, but he didn't arrive home. He fell asleep at the wheel and ended up in hospital, with his face swollen about twice normal size. He was pretty badly cut up and nearly lost his eyesight. So, Ron was out of action for about two months and from then on he switched more to management.'

By 1973, Rondel Racing had over a dozen employees and was running five F2 cars, with a driver line-up that included double World Champion Graham Hill and future champion Jody Scheckter. But by the end of that season the team's fortunes suffered a setback. Resources had been stretched through building a new factory, at Feltham, where Rondel built its own cars and was also working on a F1 car project with a view to a future entry into that category. The company's financial reserves were further depleted when its backers pulled out amid the international fuel crisis that was adversely affecting all of motorsport. So Rondel Racing was sold and its partners went their separate ways.

'Tinker' Trundle first began F1 racing in 1968 and was the original partner of Ron Dennis.

Neil Trundle went F1 racing, taking with him the Rondel F1 car, which became the basis of the Token F1 entry – a short-lived enterprise that also became a victim of inadequate funding. Neil then found gainful employment with the well-established Tyrrell F1 team and stayed there for two years, until the end of 1976. His former partner, meanwhile, having found financial support from Philip Morris through its Marlboro brand, organized and ran a succession of successful racing ventures. These included fielding front-running teams competing in F2 and F3, and also building and preparing the cars running in the BMW Procar series. Ron Dennis called his companies Projects – Rondel Racing having been Project One – and by the time Project Four came along in 1977, Neil Trundle was back working for his old friend.

'Project Four continued through to 1980,' Neil remembers, 'and we were winning championships, always putting on a good show, getting a bigger reputation. Ron brought in Creighton Brown (another successful F2 team entrant) as a financial partner. At the end of '78, I think it was, we moved into a bigger place, in Woking. All the guys decorated the new workshop and we built a mezzanine above the shop for Ron's office. We painted the floor once a month, kept everything spic and span. One of our hardest workers in those days was the team gofer, Ekrem Sami, who polished all the cars and did the odd jobs. As you know, Ekrem (now managing director of TAG McLaren Marketing Services) went on to bigger and better things. A lot of guys did, like Indy Lall, who also started as a gofer, then ran our Formula 3 team in the Project days and who runs our Test Team now. Anyway, early in '79, Ron said: "We're going F1. We're going to build our own car."'

Gary Walker was Number One mechanic for both Alain Prost and Ayrton Senna from 1988 to 1992.

John Barnard, an innovative designer then working on the Chapparal IndyCar project, was persuaded (over a three-hour dinner with Ron and Neil) to become the designer of Project Four's F1 car. A revolutionary decision was taken to build the chassis from carbon fibre, instead of the traditional aluminium honeycomb construction used by the established F1 teams. To supply the rare new material, a deal was struck with Hercules Aerospace, experts in using carbon fibre in the US space programme, and before long the F1 car had become a physical reality. To actually race it would require substantial new funding and for that Ron Dennis approached Marlboro which, for several years, had been supporting the McLaren F1 team. As the Marlboro McLarens had floundered, with no Grand Prix victories since 1977, the possibility of revitalizing the team with an injection of new blood beckoned. Thus it was decided to merge the interests of McLaren Racing and Project Four, and at the end of 1980 a new company, McLaren International, was created.

Ron Dennis was appointed joint managing director, along with Teddy Mayer, one of the founders of McLaren Racing. Also on that first board of McLaren International were John Barnard and Creighton Brown, as well as Tyler Alexander, who had helped Bruce found the original team and who is still a McLaren man, working as an engineer on the Race Team.

"It wasn't just luck, or good fortune. Through a combination of leadership, ambition and single-mindedness, Ron transformed the company into an enormously successful outfit."
John Watson
(winner of the first race for McLaren International)

One of the promises of the new regime was to win a race in 1981 and that was duly delivered when John Watson, driving the carbon fibre, Ford-powered Marlboro McLaren MP4, won the British Grand Prix. The rest, as they say, is history, and some of the current McLaren people are especially well placed to talk about it.

Combining the forces of Project Four and McLaren brought Bob McMurray into the fold. Previously, Bob had a foot in both camps, working first for Bruce McLaren as early as 1968 and then for Ron Dennis back in the Rondel days. A New Zealander (though he was born in England), Bob was fascinated by the racing life in to which so many of his countrymen (including his brother-in-law) had followed Bruce McLaren. In the beginning, when he was known as the 'Nameless Mate', Bob simply hung around the McLaren factory at Colnbrook, acting as an unpaid helper. 'It was just amazing to walk in there and see the Formula 1 car, the IndyCar and the CanAm car parked there. I just loved it. And they were such a good bunch of guys, mainly New Zealanders anyway, so I just had to be part of it.'

Bob became a jack of all trades, driving the trucks and working on the cars. Nowadays he uses his wide variety of experience to set up and look after the motorhomes and the VIP area at the races. For Bob and his wife Shaune, who until recently ran the team's main motorhome, McLaren is like a family, led by its hard-driving but benevolent patriarch.

'There's definitely a feeling of family about it,' Bob says. 'I would say there's a better team spirit at McLaren than at any other team. McLaren is and always has been a very good place to work. Before Ron it was a place people wanted to work and since Ron it's the same. Ron looks after his people remarkably well. I've known him a very long time, socializing as well as working, and I've never once regretted being involved with him. He's a good friend and a good guy.

'The first thing you need to know if you work for Ron is that you will not ever do anything shoddy on anything to do with McLaren. It's got to be done right. Many years ago, when we were working out of Maurice Gomm's place, we were going to a

One of the promises of the new regime was to win a race in 1981 and that was duly delivered when John Watson, driving the carbon fibre, Ford-powered Marlboro McLaren MP4, won the British Grand Prix.

teamwork · **the originals**

Formula 2 race, and Neil Trundle and I were pushing the car onto the back of the truck. We were late because we'd had to make up a rollbar link and to make it look good – at least what we thought looked good – we sprayed it black. Ron came along to help us load the car and spotted the black paint and said: "Why is that? It's got to be cadmium-plated like the rest of it." And we said: "It can't be, Ron. We haven't got the time to do it." And he said: "No. The car doesn't go on until it's done."

'This was about six in the evening. So by the time Neil and I got the cad-plating done it was three hours later and we had to drive all through the night instead of stopping for a rest along the way. It was annoying as hell at the time, but you just grew up with it and it's part of McLaren now. You might call it nit-picking, but it's that sort of attention to detail that transfers its way throughout the whole company. And I'll guarantee there isn't a better presented team anywhere. In the end that gives you more pride in the team you work for.

'There has traditionally been a low turnover of staff, compared to other teams, and I think that's because there's such a good feeling within McLaren all the time. Feelings ebb and flow when you go through winning three or four championships and then fall into a slump, the way we did. But people tend to stay on to try and win again, and that's exactly what we're doing. And when older people tire of racing, a lot of them go back into the factory. But they don't leave McLaren, they just leave the travelling.'

Dave Ryan "wandered into the factory one day in 1974 and has been there ever since".

Ray Grant left the travelling and is now Production Control manager at the factory. Another New Zealander, Ray started as a mechanic on McLaren's Race Team in 1976 and was immediately rewarded with James Hunt's World Championship. He stayed on the Race Team for another three years until he decided to get married. 'My impression of racing was that it was a single man's game. I'd seen too many marriages end in tears because of all the time you have to spend on the road. So I "retired" from the Race Team. But I still feel actively involved as part of the team that manufactured the car. And having worked on the Race Team I know what they're going through.'

When Ray was on the Race Team one of his workmates was Dave Ryan, yet another New Zealander possessed with those twin passions of wanderlust and a love of motorsport. Having trained as a mechanic, Dave thought he might like to try driving in speedway racing, a version of motorsport that takes place on dirt tracks and which is particularly popular in America. So, at the age of 18, and with what proved to be not enough money, Dave went to California and soon found himself stranded in San Francisco.

One day Dave saw a poster advertising a 14-day trip to London that would cost just about what remained of his finances. He decided to take the trip, rather than go back to New Zealand having accomplished nothing, and arrived in London with a view to hitchhiking around Europe for a couple of weeks. But by the time he had bought a backpack and a plastic raincoat his travel budget was so limited there was no other option but to stay in youth hostels in England. It was during that time that he saw another poster, this one advertising the British Grand Prix at Brands Hatch. Dave hitched a ride to the circuit, sneaked in under the fence and witnessed his first F1 race. He liked what he saw and wondered if he might somehow find a job in the sport. He asked around and it was suggested he should talk to the team that was particularly friendly to New Zealanders, since its founder Bruce McLaren was one of them.

'So, I wandered into the factory one day in 1974 and have been here ever since. My first job was sweeping floors and polishing the show cars. Living away from home like that – and it's still true today of Australians, New Zealanders, South Africans, what have you – racing is not just a job, it's your whole life. So you end up putting a lot of effort into it. You obviously enjoy doing it, and you're able to make the commitment you need to progress.'

Dave Ryan's commitment saw him progress from sweeper and polisher to the position of Race Team manager he has today. Over the years Dave has seen many changes at McLaren, including the level of commitment, which he thinks is greater than ever.

'We aspire to be the best team in Formula 1. It's not just an advertising spiel. It's what we believe. A huge amount of effort goes into it. We have a lot of very good people working for us and everybody, from the bottom to the top, works very hard. The way we work, our whole image, is very much down to Ron. He brought in a different level of professionalism to Formula 1, and the other teams have tried to copy it. He is a perfectionist and it can be frustrating as hell. But then, sometimes he thinks I'm as difficult as hell – although we have a good working relationship. I'm here because of Ron and I owe him a lot. We all do. I respect him enormously. I think anyone who doesn't is a fool. We can all learn a lot from Ron Dennis.'

Like Dave, the career of Inderjeet 'Indy' Lall, now the Test Team manager, began with him acting as a gofer, in his case for Ron's Project Four team. For Indy, a keen racing enthusiast who was born in Kenya and moved with his family to the UK as a boy, gofering was far beneath his ambition but it gave him the opportunity to join a top team, albeit from the bottom. Starting with Project Four in 1978 he quickly made the most of the circumstances and was rewarded with rapid advancement, though he suggests his speedy progress was at least partly due to his habit of pestering his boss for promotion.

'I kept saying to Ron, "I need to get on, I need to do this, I need to do that." And he kept saying, "Just hang on. It will happen." And it did. He made it happen and he

Indy Lall (*left*) **was Number One mechanic on Alain Prost's winning McLaren at Zandvoort in 1984.**

inspires you to make things happen. Ron is probably the most inspirational person in my life, other than my father. With Ron you learn the right way to go racing, the way generally to do any work at all, even at home. If you're decorating a room, for instance, there's nothing clever about going about your business in a messy way. If you're organized, you're more efficient and you're working in a much nicer environment.'

By 1984, Indy was Number One mechanic on Alain Prost's McLaren F1 car, though the championship that year was won by Prost's team-mate, Niki Lauda, in the final race of the season. Only a half a point separated the two drivers, yet coming so tantalizingly close to being the Number One mechanic for the number one driver in the world was not enough to keep Indy at McLaren. 'I had aspirations, and still have. I believe a lot of it is influenced by Ron, but I firmly believe that one has to always look at improving oneself, looking forward to bigger and better things.'

For Indy, this meant a move to IndyCar racing in America, where he had an offer from a team that would give him more responsibility and more money. 'So I handed my notice in to Ron and said I was going to the States. He certainly didn't want me to do it. He was very protective about McLaren and gave me all sorts of reasons why I should stay with the team. He didn't stop me, but he wouldn't accept my resignation. He said: "You're going on a vacation." And so I left.

'Unfortunately, it didn't work out. The IndyCar team's goals, their aspirations of getting success, the way they went about racing, just weren't anything like I'd experienced with Ron in Formula 1. They weren't serious enough. It was all very disappointing.'

But Indy persevered until the Indianapolis 500 race, where one of his team's cars was involved in a serious accident caused by a component failure during qualifying. Following this, Indy was crouched down in a corner of the garage, despondent and discouraged as he sifted through the wreckage of the car, when a familiar apparition came into his line of vision.

'I saw this pair of feet coming towards me and I immediately recognized them. I glanced up and, sure enough, it was Ron, standing there with a big grin on his face. And he said: "I told you so. When do you want to come back?"'

A month later. Indy was back at McLaren, sitting in the boss's office. Before Indy and his wife left for America they had rented out their house, so they now needed temporary accommodation. Indy explained their predicament to Ron, 'And he said: "No problem. We'll sort you out a house." He picked up the phone and did it, then and there. The estate agent told him they would need money up front for short-term accommodation. Ron said: "If I can pay Niki Lauda's retainer for a year I'm sure I can afford to rent your house!" A couple of hours later he handed over the keys. It was brilliant.'

Suffering through even the worst adversity, including Mika Hakkinen's serious accident in Australia in 1995, has helped draw the personnel together. But there is nothing like success to send the team spirit soaring...

Not all the memories of McLaren's Wrinklies are happy and when the subject of the worst side of motorsport – the deaths of drivers – is brought up the usually good-natured banter around their table takes on a serious note. Most agree that, after the death of Bruce McLaren, one of the worst moments in the team's history was the day in 1994 when Ayrton Senna was killed. Everyone at McLaren considered it a great privilege to work with the brilliant Brazilian, the most successful of all McLaren drivers, and even though he was driving for Williams when he died, nowhere was his loss felt more acutely than among his former team-mates.

Jo Ramirez, McLaren's team co-ordinator, was particularly close to Ayrton and still finds it difficult to mention his name. Of all the 35 victories Ayrton won for McLaren the one Jo remembers most is the 1993 Australian Grand Prix, at Adelaide, Ayrton's last race for McLaren before he moved to Williams. Jo was beside his car on the starting grid, helping him cinch up his seatbelts, when Ayrton confessed he felt very strange. 'And I said to Ayrton: "You just win this for us and we'll love you forever." He grabbed my arm, squeezed it really hard, and his eyes filled up. Mine did, too.' Jo was worried that the emotional moment might adversely affect Ayrton's performance, but it didn't. He won the race to give McLaren a record 104 Grand Prix victories – one more than Ferrari, its only rival in that department. Later, in the post-race concert at the circuit, Jo was one of the many thousands of people deeply moved when Tina

Turner pulled Ayrton onto the stage and held his hand aloft while she sang her hit song 'Simply The Best'. Jo has it on video but has never watched it.

Suffering through even the worst adversity, including Mika Hakkinen's serious accident in Australia in 1995, has helped draw the personnel together. But there is nothing like success to send the team spirit soaring and the highlight in that regard was during the 1988 season when, with Ayrton Senna and Alain Prost driving, the McLaren–Hondas won 15 of the 16 races. Neil Trundle was chief mechanic that year, and also in 1989 when the team was nearly as dominant. 'They were my two best years in racing,' he says. 'No doubt about it. The thing that really makes a difference is that kind of success, but you can't stay on top all the time. Drivers move on, you change engine suppliers, the car may not be quite right. Things are always changing, but the spirit stays. And Ron is always trying to keep morale up. When we've gone through a bad patch he would say: "Don't get down in the dumps. If I can go through these times, you can. Keep pushing and we'll come back." And when you start knocking on the door again after a dull time, there's nothing like that feeling of anticipation.'

Like most of The Wrinklies, Neil watches the races on television, though he admits his viewing is often intermittent. 'I always watch the start, but when it gets really tense – during the pit stops or when something could go wrong near the end – I have to go off and do something else, then come back when the old heartbeat has come down, or wait for the highlights that night when I know the result. I was actually quite cool when I was racing. It's much worse when you're at home watching it on TV. A few times I've watched it right the way through live, and when we're winning I'm jumping out of my seat! That's the way it is with most of the guys here. And I guess that's what it's all about, isn't it?'

On Monday mornings following a Grand Prix, in the same canteen where The Wrinklies do their reminiscing, Ron Dennis holds a debrief for as many staff that can crowd into the room. Says Neil Trundle: 'He gives a full rundown of the race, then takes questions. It really draws everybody together. The team needs Ron driving it all the time. Any time Ron doesn't drive it, I don't think we'll get the job done. And Ron always says we are all going to be here way beyond the next century!'

Ron Dennis

'This company was founded by Bruce McLaren,' Ron Dennis says. 'My name is not on the front door. I only want to be a chapter in the McLaren book.'

It may say McLaren on the door but everything about the modern organization speaks volumes for the founder's successor. The Dennis influence, his personality, values and ethics, permeate McLaren to the core. His employees never talk about the team for more than a few sentences without mentioning his name, and most media references to McLaren make its leader the central character. Based on the facts found in the record books it would not be a work of fiction to write that Ron Dennis has transformed Bruce McLaren's legacy into a legend.

In 1966, the year Bruce McLaren first entered a car bearing his name in F1 racing, Ron Dennis was beginning his career in motorsport. Two years later, when Bruce won McLaren's first Grand Prix, Ron was a mechanic on an opposing team. In 1970, the year Bruce was killed, Ron took the decision that would eventually merge his own destiny with that of McLaren.

Ron Dennis came into F1 in 1966 and joined McLaren in 1980. His influence has helped transform Bruce McLaren's legacy into a legend.

Born in Woking in 1947, Ron left school after taking his O-levels and in 1965 began an apprenticeship with Thompson & Taylor, an automotive engineering company based at the old Brooklands race circuit in nearby Byfleet. Following a take-over, the premises became the headquarters for the Cooper Car Company and Ron began working for the race car manufacturer. After a period on the production line building cars for F2 and F3 racing, Ron was transferred to the Cooper F1 team, where, in 1966 and just over 18 years old, he went to his first race – the Mexican Grand Prix – as a mechanic on the Cooper driven by the Austrian Jochen Rindt. When Rindt moved to Brabham for the 1968 season Ron went with him as his personal mechanic. In 1969 Rindt left Brabham for Lotus (and was killed at the 1970 Italian Grand Prix), but Ron stayed at Brabham, where he became chief mechanic and where the flash of inspiration occurred that set him on course for the position he holds today.

While the Brabham cars were being shipped from the US Grand Prix to the last race of the 1970 season, in Mexico, Ron had a few days' holiday in Acapulco. There, lying beside a pool in the Mexican sun, he contemplated his future. Though just 23 years old, he was in charge of preparing the Brabham cars, looking after much of the team's business affairs, even handling the prize money. Despite feeling somewhat over-awed by the responsibility, Ron suddenly realized he was doing everything necessary to run a team yet only drawing a salary for it. And so, he thought, 'Why not run my own team?'

The Dennis influence, his personality, values and ethics, permeate McLaren to the core. His employees never talk about the team for more than a few sentences without mentioning his name...

Once his mind was made up, the several characteristics that became his trademark were applied to forming his team. Among them was an obsession with cleanliness. As a mechanic, Ron hated getting his clothes soiled and his hands dirty, and within half an hour of going home at night he had scrubbed himself spotlessly clean. He treated racing cars similarly. With his conviction that just because something was mechanical it didn't have to be dirty, after each race Ron had what he called a 'Dirty Day', when he would spend hours taking a car apart, meticulously cleaning every single component, then re-assembling it. The cleaning up process he disliked, but systematically putting the car back together again gave him great satisfaction, as did the pleasure of admiring the gleaming finished product. Top-quality presentation became a cornerstone of his team-building philosophy, as did the pursuit of excellence, which he approached with the same zeal lavished on his racing cars.

Brought into play was a passion for precision and an almost fanatical attention to detail. There were also an intense power of concentration, an unwavering determination to succeed and a relentless ambition to push that success beyond established frontiers. Any high-profile authority figure possessed with such a combination of potentially aggressive personality traits risks being labelled something rather less than loveable. Ron's steely resolve can be intimidating and outsiders having occasional contact with his self-admitted often stern presence have called him cold, abrasive, egotistical, aloof, arrogant – characteristics that have also been attributed to his team.

Yet throughout McLaren scarcely a disparaging word can be heard about Ron Dennis. Instead, there is universal admiration and respect. Within the team he is regarded, at worst, as a benevolent dictator and, by those who know him best, as a caring and sensitive man. Rather than abusing his position of power he has taken advantage of it on numerous occasions to help employees, friends, even F1 rivals, sort out personal difficulties. If he has a failing, some contend, it is an overly developed sense of loyalty that makes him reluctant to make redundant anyone who may no longer be contributing adequately to the team effort. Most of all, the McLaren people say, he is an inspirational leader and a motivator of the highest order.

Just where all of this comes from, the man himself is not sure. As a boy, the future leader of men noted for his fierce competitiveness and seemingly inexhaustible stamina, bred rabbits as a hobby and shunned competitive sports. On reflection, he admits there were certain telling moments in his formative years when the seeds might have been sown that blossomed into a deep determination to achieve very high ambitions. Several times his admittedly lofty pronouncements of what he might one day become when he grew up were greeted by his older brother and his schoolmates with derisory comments and hoots of laughter. I'll show them, Ron thought.

'You see, I have always believed that if you really want to do something, you can do it. It's like climbing a mountain of ambition. If things out of your control have an influence on the path you take, you can fall off. Some people get catapulted up the mountain by an amazing stroke of good fortune. But by and large, if you've climbed up the mountain in a sure-footed way and reached the summit, the path you have taken brings into your character one essential ingredient that allows you to stay on top: a wealth of experience. With that experience you can build on your successes and go beyond previous limits. I just don't think you have a limit. The possibilities are limitless.'

His hard climb to the top was not without its pitfalls. In 1972, while operating Rondel Racing with his partner Neil Trundle, Ron worked himself into a state of exhaustion preparing the cars for an F2 race and fell asleep at the wheel while driving his E-type Jaguar. In the crash he received severe facial lacerations (repaired by plastic surgery) and a serious eye injury that put him out of commission for two months. Typically, he turned this negative into a positive. 'In fact, it was probably the most positive thing that ever happened to me because it pulled me into management. We employed another mechanic to do my job and I ran the team. That was the big starting point.'

For Ron, there is no finishing point because, as he is fond of saying, 'to stand still in motor racing is to go backwards'. To make rapid progress – from Rondel through to his Project Two, Three and Four teams – he concentrated on developing comprehensive professionalism, highlighted by immaculate preparation and presentation. The factory floors were painted frequently, the teams brought a signwriter to the circuits to touch up the paintwork on the complex colour schemes of the cars and the truck driver was instructed to park in the paddock so that the names on the tyres were all pointing precisely in the same direction.

At that time, when the commercial potential of motor racing was in its infancy, the Dennis-run teams were well ahead of the competition and Ron's reputation escalated accordingly. Among those impressed was McLaren's then main sponsor Philip Morris, which arranged a merger with Project Four as a cure for the doldrums in which Marlboro McLaren had floundered for several years. Thus, at the age of 34, Ron joined McLaren to start the 1981 season and the record of success that followed is a direct result of the goals he set.

McLaren's stated goal is to win every F1 race. It hasn't achieved that, but it has come closer than most and when it comes to the total number of victories its main rival is Ferrari. Both teams passed the 100 Grands Prix win mark some time ago but the famous Italian team, having entered the World Championship series when it was first organized in 1950, had a 16-year head start on McLaren. Over three-quarters of McLaren's wins have come since Ron took over, and while the team has occasionally

teamwork · **the originals**

faltered during his tenure it has seldom looked anything less than a potential winner. Even during the drought of 50 races without a win (1994 to 1996), rival front-running teams watched their mirrors expectantly for McLaren's inevitable return to the forefront. According to Ron, a main reason why McLaren is such a perennial powerhouse is 'attention to detail'.

'Every single detail is important. You break down the whole Grand Prix scenario into the tiniest details. Individually, you might barely perceive them, hardly measure them. But you look at each of these facets and try to improve them. Those little improvements add up to considerable improvement.

'You have to start with the really fundamental basics. When someone walks into a room I notice straightaway such details as fingernails, whether they are cleaned and manicured, how the person is dressed, whether they're scruffy or neat and tidy. If you don't have respect for your own body, then I think you tend to lack personal discipline.'

Listening to Ron talk is like being persuasively lectured on the art of winning.

Ron's legendary personal discipline (which includes a steady regimen of 14-hour days in his office, interrupted by travels to the races, where he goes to 'relax') is matched by a continual quest for self-improvement, especially for the acquisition of knowledge. While at school he was not a diligent student, though his subsequent development of his intellect and the eloquence with which he can express it – through 'Ronspeak', which is sometimes ridiculed for its complexity, but never for the profundity of its content – would now easily enable him to stand tall in the halls of academe. Certainly, he could write the definitive textbook on how to create and run a successful F1 team. And listening to him talk is like being persuasively lectured on the art of winning.

'Built into my management approach is a commitment to many philosophies that I believe are important to maintaining and perpetuating a successful company. My

knowledge comes from a commitment to excellence, to learn and understand those elements that can contribute to the process of success. That can range from attending management and motivational seminars, reading management books and magazines (such as *The Harvard Business Week* and *The Economist*), wrestling with the concept of lateral thinking (influenced by the concept's inventor, Edward de Bono) and working hard to understand people.

'I think the software of the company, its human resources, is absolutely vital to success. So we put a great emphasis on keeping our human resource quotient in its optimum frame of mind. We go into great detail to create the right working environment. This includes such things as carefully choosing the colour scheme for our offices and factory, maintaining the correct temperature and humidity, cleanliness, lighting, even the smell – we have used fragrances in our working environment. If you go into a room that is smelling of dirty coffee cups, has dirty windows and wilting flowers your mind-set is completely different from going into a clean, well-lit and pleasant-smelling room.'

That room, indeed McLaren's entire corporate colour scheme, will inevitably reflect variations on the theme of the team leader's favourite colour.

'The problem with grey is that people immediately see it as a colour that goes with blandness. But I see it as a colour that works very well in mixtures and hues and responds to highlights. I like the flexibility of grey and I didn't choose it by accident. I think it's fresh, clean and has a tranquil effect, and it's also got dignity and class.

'I believe strongly in personal discipline, which leads to accountability and accepting responsibility, which are all important in a negative situation. The allocation of blame in a failure situation is just a complete waste of time. The most important thing is to recognize the mistake and rectify it fast.

'Running this business is not easy and it does require some ruthlessness, which is the hard part of management. It doesn't happen often, but I believe that having to

left: **Ron's steady regimen of 14-hour days in the office is interrupted by travels to the races, where he goes to "relax".**

fire someone is my failure, not theirs, because it means they shouldn't have been hired in the first place. When you really successfully grapple with understanding people's characters you find their strengths and weaknesses, which enables you to build on their strengths and support their weaknesses. I think a huge percentage of management in this world use the weakness of an individual as a mechanism for attempting to obtain loyalty and commitment. That's a badly used technique because it's basically running your company through intimidation and fear.

"Whether you're winning or not winning, there is no solution other than hard work. Not just the physical, but also the thought processes."

'It is rarely an enjoyable experience being the boss. Ninety-nine per cent of the individuals who come to see me in my office, or telephone me, are people with problems who are passing them on to me to handle. They rarely say "Isn't this a beautiful day" or "This is a wonderful place to work", though I take some encouragement from the fact that not many say they are unhappy at McLaren. But there are moments of great satisfaction. A well-executed contract has a certain warmth to it, and when you wake up in the morning the day after a successful Grand Prix, that has a particular warmth to it.'

Ron is a sore loser and has admitted feeling physical pain on the Monday morning after not winning a Grand Prix. Failure to succeed only inspires him to try harder and at the start of every day he hits the ground running.

'There is a very brief period, that lasts from the moment I wake up to the moment my feet hit the floor at the side of the bed, that is just about the only amount of time I have where I could not be motivated. When things aren't working and you want them to work you either allow it to demotivate or motivate yourself. If I'm not motivated there is absolutely no possibility of me motivating the rest of the people in the company.

'So, a fundamental requirement of being the head of the company is to be the prime motivating force. What you hope to do with all the people around you is develop a good positive attitude so that you're not alone in the process. And we've got people who have been with us for years and years who have a conviction that when things go wrong everything will eventually come right. We've had problems in the past and worked them out. Motivation is a strange but essential ingredient in the process of winning. You would think that it struggles in adversity, but it's the opposite. When you are winning everything, then motivation becomes a major issue. Whether you're winning or not winning, there is no solution other than hard work. Not just the physical, but also the thought processes.'

Ron has developed his thinking powers to a very high degree and to illustrate the mind-set necessary to think productively he draws an analogy to a sprinter preparing for a 100 metre race.

'A sprinter has total concentration on what he is about to do. And just think of the kind of advantage you can have if you train yourself to apply that level of concentration on an hour-to-hour basis. Thinking is a very cheap commodity. The only thing it's costing you is time, but in the end well-considered creative thought processes will save you time. So, you train yourself to think in a disciplined way, playing a kind of mental three-dimensional chess to make sure you've covered all the options to solve the many complex issues there are in this business. You really have to keep your mind focused and watch that everything functions in an optimum way. It can be very wearing, very fatiguing, and take all emotion out of me.'

Ron is a sore loser and has admitted to feeling physical pain on the Monday morning after not winning a Grand Prix.

In Ron's mind there is no room for negative thoughts, because they are non-productive and a waste of energy. He has become a master at positive thinking and also at controlling his emotions, in the belief that the extremes at either end of the emotional scale are obstacles on the route to success. He has developed enough mental strength to at least keep depression at bay, if not eliminate it, and he also thinks it necessary to keep a careful check on 'non-productive and non-professional' displays of elation.

David Coulthard and many in the team wept with emotion when he won the 1997 Australian Grand Prix, ending a lengthy period without a McLaren victory. There were also widespread tears when Mika Hakkinen won his first F1 race at the end of that

"I won't even consider stopping my involvement in the Grand Prix team until we've won more World Championships. Not even one more will fit the bill." *Ron Dennis*

season. Though the team leader hugged his drivers and briefly exhibited a broad grin on these momentous occasions he was less demonstrably affected because 'when you see a doctor delivering a baby you don't see him jumping up and down. He has a professional approach to something that is an emotional moment. That's the way we want to be. The moment you stop being professional is the moment you start the downward spiral to failure.'

Though he disapproves of 'this enthusiastic schoolboy reaction' to getting the job done that you are supposed to do, he also believes in wholesale celebrations of success at the appropriate time and place. At the annual McLaren Christmas party over 1000 people disport themselves in joyous fashion, none more so than the managing director of the TAG McLaren Group.

Ron talks about how F1 puts people into a 'sort of personality showcase' and when facial expressions are closely scrutinized to provide clues to personality traits the wrong impression can be given. When he permits himself the occasional grin, 'people say I'm smug. If I walk around with my normal scowl they say I'm miserable.' When his demeanour is mostly sombre, 'I'm thought of as dull and boring. But it's because

Ron tries, not always successfully, to keep non-productive emotions in check.

I'm thinking hard and want to devote all my thought processes to concentrate on the job at hand.'

While Ron is deep in thought in the inner sanctum of his office at headquarters he is shielded from unnecessary interruptions by his two personal assistants. He says they act as a kind of filtration system on his business hours and, along with his wife Lisa, his PAs Beverly Keynes and Justine Blake are the only people able to read Ron's mind and assess his mood.

'He doesn't have huge mood swings,' says Justine Blake, who has been a PA to Ron since 1993, 'even though he's in such a high-stress situation where things can go wrong from time to time. He amazes me in that instead of becoming irritable, upset or annoyed, he rises above it. People say he's cold, because he doesn't seem to show emotion even when something fabulous happens, although I can tell the difference between the normal Ron, the happy Ron and the upset Ron.'

With her degree in Politics, Justine might have chosen a more conventional career, but the stimulation of working for Ron Dennis is 'brilliant! I get a real buzz from it. When he's working flat out, or when there's a crisis going on, I get an adrenaline rush. The pace gets quicker, and he'll go faster and faster until you're quite dizzy. But if I forget something or make a mistake, he'll quietly remind me. He will never snap at me. If he was snappy or aggressive I would be very stressed. But because he is so cool in the way he conducts himself on a day-to-day basis, it keeps me calm and I can do my job better. And he is very, very clever. You can never double-guess him. He's always interesting to listen to and he has a very charismatic personality.'

Justine Blake, seen here talking to Mark Arnall, is a personal assistant and one of the few people seemingly able to read Ron's mind and assess his mood.

Justine, like most in the team, talks about McLaren being a big family, albeit a very hard-working one. And that intense, demanding, no-nonsense, nose-to-the-grindstone approach contributes to perceptions about the limitations of the McLaren family's personality, as the patriarch acknowledges.

'If people say we look sterile and unemotional from the outside, I do think there is a level of warmth and commitment to each other that you can only feel on the inside. We have a personality that I hope reflects honesty, integrity, focus. We are also seen as predatory, a word I quite like. We carefully stalk and systematically approach our prey – which is winning a race. That aggressive approach to our goal is tempered by values within the company where we are caring, supportive, loyal to our employees.

'I think the thing that makes McLaren successful is that it is a very successful team, and "team" is the key word. My role in that team is to put it together, making sure that all the political, promotional and organizational considerations marry. I have to package the elements and make it a team effort. It's a knitting together of egos, likes, dislikes, motivating forces, things that destabilize, things that harmonize. Having the ability to try and dissect all these things and then getting them to mesh together, I'd like to think that's what I'm reasonably competent at.'

An important part of meshing together the personnel at McLaren is the policy of name-calling, whereby everyone is known by their first name, including the team leader. 'The philosophy behind that is quite simple. I've always worked on a first-name basis because no matter who you are – the prime minister of Great Britain, the chief executive of the largest company in the world, the guy who sweeps the floor in the factory – when you get up in the morning you put one leg in one trouser leg and one in the other. You are a human being like everybody else. And what's important when you make contact with people is that there are no barriers.

While Ron is deep in thought in the inner sanctum of his office at headquarters he is shielded from unnecessary interruptions by his two personal assistants.

'Calling everybody by their first name breaks down barriers. The respect people have for each other should come from their ability to do their job well, not from their position in the company, their rank, their title or their name. Besides, it's difficult to remember every name now that there are some 750 of us in the Group. So we provide clothes with our names on them, on the Race Team and now in the factory as well. We are not a colony of ants. We are a group of hard-working individuals with a common objective, and wearing the company uniform is a great morale-booster and team-builder.'

Building the team, boosting its morale, putting so much effort into managing it, must surely be a stressful occupation. How does Ron handle stress? 'I don't have it. It's not a productive emotion. Maybe I've learned to channel stress into adrenaline. I certainly have masses of adrenaline. Without doubt, the most relaxing part of my

workweek is going to a Grand Prix. It is far less complex than sitting behind my desk dealing with the mountains of paperwork and solving all the inevitable problems that come my way. At times I have even thought that the management in the company was showering me with memos and problems in written form in order to keep me behind my desk and not interfere with them running the business!

'Motor racing is an absolutely essential motivational force in my life. I love it. I love the adrenaline. I love the challenge. I love the competition. But more than I love those things I love this company, and I have to be responsible for it. There are many people who depend on McLaren for their livelihood, and many other people in the other companies within the Group have similar needs.'

At the end of his long working days there is precious little time left for Ron to devote to the most important people in his life: his wife Lisa and their growing children, Charlie, Christian and Francesca. To free himself to have more time for his family was one of the reasons he chose to take on the managing director's role of the Group, but he seems busier than ever. How much longer can he continue his current pace?

'Many more years. That's as accurate as I can be. Certainly, I won't even consider stopping my involvement in the Grand Prix team until we've won more World Championships. Not even one more will fit the bill. But you have to provide an

Motor racing is an absolutely essential motivational force in Ron's life (seen here with Steve Hallam).

insurance policy for the what-ifs of this world: "What if I fall under a bus? What if I choose to retire?" – neither of which I have any intention of doing. I feel it is my responsibility to make sure something solid is there to perpetuate the growth of the company and the Group as a whole.'

With F1 racing as the catalyst, Ron is taking the TAG McLaren Group in new directions. On the racing side he has started a Driver Support Programme to foster and develop future F1 driving talent. Six young drivers, two of them just 12 years old, are being given financial and technical backing in karting, F3 and F3000 racing.

'The Driver Support Programme, which we have put together with Mercedes, has been designed to create genuine support for drivers who, without the commercial horsepower we can bring, may not have made it on their own. To be in the programme, above all else, you have to be exceptionally talented, focused and capable of winning races.'

Speaking of the youngsters in karting, Ron notes that their racing activities won't come at the expense of their education. 'I think it is important that we not only guide and support them financially, but make sure that they maintain their schooling. I will see their reports from school to be quite sure they are keeping up academically, because you have to be a completely rounded individual to succeed in motorsport.'

Ron's most ambitious current project – one of the largest private construction projects in Europe – is building a new corporate headquarters/technology centre for the TAG McLaren Group. Located on a 49 hectare site on the outskirts of Woking, the new 35,500 square metre facility will bring the Group's various companies, currently housed in 16 different buildings, under one roof by the year 2001. Designed by a team of architects led by the world-renowned Sir Norman Foster, the corporate headquarters will house an automotive research centre, an education centre and a museum, as well as McLaren International, McLaren Cars, TAG Electronic Systems, TAG McLaren Marketing Services and, of course, Ron's main source of inspiration, McLaren International – his beloved race team.

"You win Grands Prix and World Championships not by what you are doing with regards to the next race, or even the race after that. You do it by what you have planned for the future. And the future is infinite."
Ron Dennis

left: **Ron, with Mansour, is taking the TAG Group in new directions.**

Since 1985 Ron's silent partner has been Mansour Ojjeh, head of the parent TAG Group that owns 60 per cent of the empire Ron has built. Educated in Egypt, Switzerland, America and France, Mansour is a sophisticated man of the world and a businessman *par excellence*. Among his many business interests the stimulation Mansour gets from his McLaren involvement is especially rewarding and he thinks his partner who runs it deserves all the credit he gets.

'A lot of people ask why it's always Ron, Ron, Ron, and not me. Some people think Ron is pompous. But they don't understand him. You have to get to know him. He's very disciplined but he likes to have a good time when he can. He's a great manager. Fine, so he's had our backing, but the success of McLaren is down to him. He is probably THE professional in F1 today. He's more than just the manager of a team. He's a businessman, a figurehead and sometimes a diplomat. He's got a very good entrepreneurial mind and has great foresight.'

In his career to date, Ron has come a long way and brought a lot of people with him. He has become a very wealthy man and he shares the wealth – the McLaren employees are probably the best paid in the business. He is a racer and also a businessman and when discussing the relative satisfaction he gets from both pursuits there is no question where his heart lies.

'Obviously, satisfaction comes from the performance of the company, the racing performance and the commercial performance. Our fiscal performance I think is quite impressive, considering the size of the company, the number of people, the fact that it's a private company. But we don't drive any of our companies on profit. We drive them on a clear-cut desire to be the best. And if you have a premium product the profit will come.

'The driving force has got to be a desire to be the best, not just to make money. Fortunately, if you are winning Grands Prix you can have both. I've often said I would prefer to be recognized as a successful businessman before a successful motorsport director. But if it came to a choice, I would most certainly choose winning a Grand Prix over making a million dollars.'

right: **Ron is successful in both business and racing. But there is no question where his heart lies.**

1963 Bruce McLaren forms Bruce McLaren Motor Racing Limited.

1966 The McLaren M2B Ford makes its F1 debut, at the Monaco Grand Prix, with Bruce McLaren driving.

1968 McLaren wins its first F1 race, the Belgian Grand Prix, with Bruce McLaren driving.

1970 Sadly, Bruce McLaren is killed while testing a CanAm sportscar at Goodwood.

1970-74 McLaren cars continue to win in F1, IndyCar and CanAm racing.

1974 Team McLaren enters a commercial partnership with Philip Morris, through its leading brand Marlboro. The Marlboro McLaren M23 -Ford wins both the F1 Drivers' World Championship, with Emerson Fittipaldi, and the Constructors' World Championship, symbolic of team supremacy.

1976 James Hunt wins the Drivers' World Championship in the Marlboro McLaren M23 Ford.

1980 McLaren International is established, with the merger of McLaren and Project Four, a successful British racing company led by Ron Dennis.

1981 The first victory for the new team, with John Watson driving the Marlboro McLaren MP/4 Ford in the British Grand Prix. It is McLaren's 25th win and the first in F1 for an all carbon fibre chassis.

1984 McLaren forms a partnership with the Techniques d'Avant Garde Group (TAG) to develop the new Porsche turbo-charged engine. The Marlboro McLaren MP4/2 TAG Porsche Turbo dominates the season, winning a record 12 of the 16 races and securing both the Drivers' Championship, with Niki Lauda beating his team mate Alain Prost by half a point, and the Constructors' Championship. Shell joins the team as fuel and lubricant supplier.

1985 McLaren wins both World Championships again, with Alain Prost securing the Drivers' title in the Marlboro McLaren MP4/2B TAG Porsche Turbo. The TAG Group becomes a major shareholder in McLaren International.

1986 Alain Prost wins his second driving title, with the McLaren MP4/2C TAG Turbo.

1987 McLaren moves into new headquarters at Woking. On display in the entrance are trophies awarded for the team's 54 Grand Prix victories to date, and also several of the cars that scored the 29 wins achieved since the formation of McLaren International. TAG McLaren Marketing Services is

1

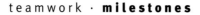

5

formed, to provide marketing, creative, communications and management services for the team and its commercial partners.

1988 With Honda as engine supplier, McLaren dominates the F1 season, winning a record 15 of 16 races. Ayrton Senna joins the team and wins his first Drivers' World Championship, in the Marlboro McLaren MP4/4. Senna takes 13 pole positions and wins eight races to establish new F1 records. His team mate Alain Prost is second to give McLaren its fourth Constructors' Championship.

1989 TAG Electronic Systems is formed to provide electronic systems for the Race Team and for road car applications. McLaren Cars is formed to create and produce the ultimate high-performance road car, the McLaren F1.

1989-91 McLaren wins three successive Constructors' World Championships, while Alain Prost, in 1989, and Ayrton Senna, in 1990 and 1991, win the Drivers' Championships in Honda-powered McLarens.

1993 Ayrton Senna's victory in the Brazilian Grand Prix in the Marlboro McLaren MP4/8 Ford is the 100th for McLaren. Senna's fifth win of the season, at the Australian Grand Prix, is the 104th for McLaren (in its 28th season), enabling the team to overtake Ferrari's record (established in 43 seasons) as the most successful constructor in F1 history. Mika Hakkinen makes his debut with the team at the Portuguese Grand Prix. McLaren arranges to use Peugeot engines for the 1994 season.

1995 McLaren enters a long-term partnership with Mercedes–Benz as engine supplier and the team finishes fourth in the Constructors' Championship. Mobil replaces Shell as fuel and lubricant supplier.

1996 With David Coulthard joining Mika Hakkinen in the Marlboro McLaren MP4/11 Mercedes, the team takes six podium finishes during the season to finish fourth in the Constructors' Championship.

1997 Reemtsma, through its leading brand West, enters a long-term partnership with McLaren. The Constructors' points scored in the Brazilian Grand Prix bring McLaren's total to 2003.5, a record for an F1 team. The West McLaren Mercedes MP4/12 wins the Australian, Italian and European Grands Prix to bring McLaren's total to 107 wins. The team finishes fourth in the Constructors' Championship, with David Coulthard and Mika Hakkinen third and sixth, respectively, in the Drivers' Championship.

1998 Bridgestone becomes the team's tyre supplier. Driving the new West McLaren Mercedes MP4/13, Mika and David begin the season by dominating the races.

6

7

1 Bruce McLaren and Tyler Alexander (right), who is still with the team. **2** 1966: Monaco – Bruce debuts the first McLaren. **3** 1968: Belgium – Bruce wins the team's first race. **4** 1968: Belgium – Bruce and Denny Hulme. **5** 1974: Emerson Fittipaldi, the team's first World Champion. **6** 1988: Portugal – the year the team won a record 15 of 16 races. **7** Between them Alain Prost and Ayrton Senna shared six World Championships with the team.

the engine

"You must admit that an engine made up of nearly 6000 parts, weighing less than 110 kilos and developing over 750 horsepower at over 17,000rpm is a beautiful piece of technology."

NORBERT HAUG
(Head of Mercedes–Benz Motorsport)

Mercedes–Benz

Mercedes–Benz, the team's engine partner, has a history that began with the invention of the horseless carriage itself – a momentous occurrence that is credited to Karl Benz, an engineer and factory owner in Mannheim, Germany. On 29 January 1886, Herr Benz was issued a patent (number 37435) for 'a vehicle with gas engine drive' which he called the Benz Patent–Motorwagen. Its first public test took place on 3 July that year on a road in Mannheim, where Karl Benz presided proudly over the proceedings as his pioneering three-wheeled device putt-putted its way into automotive legend.

A small crowd watched transfixed as the wooden chassis tricycle began to move under its own power – rated at the equivalent of 0.9 of what one plodding horse might produce – provided by the single cylinder engine which displaced 984 cubic centimetres and ran on petroleum spirit, which Herr Benz purchased from a local pharmacy. Gathering momentum and scattering the startled onlookers (and their horses), the Benz Patent–Motorwagen began to cover the ground at an astonishing rate of speed, finally reaching its maximum velocity of 16kph, amid clouds of dust and smoke and loud cheering from the enthralled spectators.

Mika Hakkinen, Jurgen Hubbert (member of the board of Mercedes–Benz) and David Coulthard continue the Mercedes tradition that began over a century ago in the first ever motor race.

Nearby, at Cannstatt, and at nearly the same time, another engineer, Gottlieb Daimler, began conducting trials with a 'motor carriage' of his own design. The Daimler Motorkutsche also had a small single cylinder engine but its chassis had four wheels, the configuration that soon replaced the tricycle as the automotive norm. Daimler's contribution to Mercedes history also included originating the three-pointed star, which represented his pursuit of solutions to travel by mechanical means on land, in the sea and in the air.

Gottlieb Daimler soon turned his inventive mind to the motoring competition that inevitably sprang up between rival manufacturers. It has always required only a difference of opinion to set the stage for a race: to prove one competitor faster than another. In the case of the horseless carriage the first ever race took place in France, on 22 July 1894, over a route of public roads between Paris and Rouen. The historic event was dominated by Daimlers which – powered by 954cc V2 engines that never skipped a beat while averaging 20.5kph – finished in the first four places.

From the beginning, the sport of motor racing helped to sell automobiles to consumers who were impressed by their prowess in competition. One of Daimler–Moteren–Gesellschaft's first customers was Emil Jellinek, a wealthy Viennese businessman who resided in Nice and fancied himself as a race driver. In 1899, Jellinek drove a four-cylinder Daimler Phoenix to victory in the Tour de Nice race. It was the custom at that time for aristocratic drivers to race under pseudonyms and Jellinek chose to call himself 'Mercedes', the Spanish name he had given to his favourite daughter. Inspired by his racing success behind the wheel of the Daimler Phoenix, Jellinek placed an order for 36 examples of the marque, with the proviso that they should be named after his daughter. In 1902, Daimler patented the Mercedes trademark, a name that soon came to symbolize automotive excellence with a sporting flourish.

The Mercedes–Benz three-pointed star was designed to show the pursuit of solutions to travel by mechanical means on land, on the sea and in the air.

The companies founded by Karl Benz and Gottlieb Daimler, who never actually met, manufactured automobiles independently until the organizations merged in 1926 to become Daimler–Benz. From its headquarters in Stuttgart, the company continued to capitalize on its racing heritage, with sporting versions of its cars speeding through the years, adding lustre to the image with ever-increasing racing success. In 1934 that image took on a silver hue, when the soon-to-become famous Daimler–Benz W125 Grand Prix cars appeared for that season's first race slightly overweight, according to the regulations. To pare them down to the minimum weight of 750kg, the team manager, Alfred Neubauer, ordered the white paint to be stripped from the cars. When the paint was removed it laid bare the gleaming silver of the aluminium chassis, thus providing the colour that became the basis for the legend of the mighty Mercedes–Benz 'Silver Arrows'.

Driven by such illustrious names as Rudolph Carracciola, Manfred von Brauchitsch, Hermann Lang, Karl Kling, Juan Manuel Fangio and Stirling Moss, the Silver Arrows cars stormed their way through racing history and into the record books, both before and after the Second World War.

In 1952, when Mercedes resumed its racing activities after the war, it was initially in sportscar events and not in Formula 1, the category of international Grand Prix events which was first formally organized into the series for the World Championship in 1950. When Mercedes did enter F1 for the 1954 season success was immediate, with the World Championship going to the great Juan Manuel Fangio in his 8 cylinder, 2.4 litre Mercedes. During the next season, Mercedes cars won five of the six Grands Prix races (held in Argentina, Monaco, Belgium, Holland, Great Britain and Italy) and Fangio (with four wins) and Stirling Moss (one win) finished first and second in the 1955 World Championship. Sadly, that season was marred by a tragic accident that claimed many lives in the Le Mans 24 hour sportscar race. A Mercedes was involved and at this point the company chose to suspend its racing activities.

Beyond the publicity factor was the practical value to be gained from engineering developments and technical feedback that might ultimately benefit Mercedes road cars.

When Mercedes went racing again, beginning in 1988, it was initially in touring cars and sportscars – branches of motorsport where several more championships were won for both Mercedes and its drivers. In 1993, the company made an exploratory return to F1 by supporting the Swiss-based Sauber team, which used engines bearing the logo 'concept by Mercedes–Benz'. For the 1994 season, Mercedes decided to make a serious return to single-seater racing, this time as a fully fledged engine supplier to teams competing in both the American-based IndyCar series and in F1 racing, the international category acknowledged as the pinnacle of motorsport. The IndyCar involvement, with the Penske team, resulted in a victory in the Mercedes engine's first race, the prestigious Indianapolis 500.

For its return to F1 Mercedes took the view that the modern version of the sport, with its enormous international audience, was the ideal sporting platform on which to

demonstrate the company's engineering capabilities and competitive spirit. Beyond the publicity factor was the practical value to be gained from engineering developments and technical feedback that might ultimately benefit Mercedes road cars.

For Mercedes engineers and technicians, F1 would provide first-hand experience in the high-speed learning process necessary to keep pace in the relentlessly competitive F1 arena. And for the 180,000 Mercedes employees around the world, being represented in competition at the highest level of motorsport would boost morale and lead to a greater sense of a team effort. Thus, on 28 October 1994 – in a year when the company was celebrating the 100th anniversary of its success in the world's first motor race – Mercedes–Benz announced the formation of a long-term partnership with McLaren to contest the FIA Formula 1 World Championship.

The famed Mercedes Silver Arrows (demonstrated here by McLaren's 1974 World Champion, Emerson Fittipaldi) stormed their way through motor racing history.

Representing Mercedes in the alliance with McLaren, and in all its motorsport activities, is Nobert Haug, whose background as an automotive journalist in Germany makes him especially conscious of the communications role F1 racing plays in the company's policy.

'F1 is really about overall image. It is a very tough playing field but for an automobile manufacturer probably the best playing field to show competence in terms of sport, in terms of comparisons with your rivals, and this way you can communicate to your customers and to your future customers. We have a strategic approach to it and use it as a marketing tool, and we communicate to much younger people now. I was not born a Mercedes guy, I was a journalist. And when they chose me I think that showed what Mercedes wants to achieve. They realize that the best technician in the world doesn't necessarily have the key to the communication issue, so why not take a communications guy and make him responsible for all of it?'

Besides being the official Mercedes communicator, Norbert sees his role as that of a player in a team. 'The key thing is that we are part of a team and each part is as important as the other. I don't have to tell the team how to win races. They know that. I have to give them support. I have to make sure that the engines are working, that we have the right budget, and that everything works smoothly between Mercedes, Ilmor and McLaren. I provide the balance. It is like trying to find the perfect set-up on the car. I also like to be able to provide some response for the drivers. They have a hell of a job to do and it's really important to help them.'

right: **Norbert Haug, head of Mercedes–Benz Motorsport, has a tremendous enthusiasm for cars and competition.**

When Norbert Haug was appointed head of Mercedes–Benz Motorsport in 1990, he brought to his job a tremendous enthusiasm for cars

teamwork · **the engine**

and competition that began when he was a small boy, probably as soon as he heard 'the noises of the cars'. Though neither of his parents drove a car, Norbert confesses that by the time he started school 'I was a maniac for cars. I loved everything about them, and I still do.'

So, too, does the Mercedes press officer, Wolfgang Schattling, who grew up in a small village near the mighty Nurburgring, the daunting German circuit where the great F1 cars and their heroic drivers from the past were put to the ultimate test. Watching them in action Wolfgang resolved one day to become involved in the sport that sent chills up and down his spine. That opportunity came in 1990 when he joined Mercedes, two months after Norbert Haug. Prior to that Wolfgang was a school teacher, specializing in English, and he also wrote occasional race reports for German magazines. As a Mercedes employee Wolfgang's job as press officer is made easier with success, but as a racing enthusiast he knows that fans of the sport must also deal with disappointment. The key for Mercedes in its relationship with the fans through the media is to balance these twin realities, as Wolfgang notes.

Talking to Mika is Mercedes press officer Wolfgang Schattling, who grew up watching races at the mighty Nurburgring.

'You can create support not only when you are successful but, what is no less important, you can gain the understanding of the media if something goes wrong. If the media knows what's going on, the reasons for both good and bad performances, they tend to be more understanding and treat it in a more positive way. That doesn't mean they don't criticize, but when you give them all the information necessary, you are treated more fairly.'

When it comes to communicating the Mercedes message to the media Norbert Haug believes in the direct approach, a concept that was fostered during his days as an F1 journalist. Norbert did not enjoy 'waiting hours for the big stars, and that's why we try to be very open and help the media. We need the communication. We don't hide.' At the Saturday afternoon media conference on race weekends, which is hosted by Wolfgang Schattling (and assisted by Anna Guerrier), Norbert Haug and Ron Dennis answer questions with a candidness that is rare in F1. When their partnership began, many of the media queries were related to the high expectations associated with the joint venture between two of the most successful names in racing.

As Norbert says: 'The expectations were huge and there was a lot of pressure on us. From the Mercedes side I made a lot of effort at that time to describe goals that were realistic. The first season, in 1995, was quite a tough one for the relationship. But as we found out, every negative has a lot of positives: '95 was a learning year for us all; '96 showed an upward trend and had some highlights; '97 was quite good and we could have done even better without our technical troubles, which were mainly engine issues in that year.

below: **Norbert Haug and Ilmor's Mario Illien were under great pressure to produce a winning partnership – and they delivered.**

'The turning point was when we won that first race in Melbourne in '97. It was amazing the kind of coverage we got. We got a lot of sheer, honest appreciation. Probably everybody in the paddock came and congratulated us. It meant a lot and it was the proof that when you start getting good results you get total credibility. People trust in you and you can build from a new level.'

right: **On race weekends Wolfgang hosts a media conference where Norbert and Ron answer questions with a candidness rare in F1.**

Accompanying the technical progress that brought about steady improvement was a strengthening of the partnership between Mercedes and McLaren, a relationship that Norbert believes has its foundations in people as much as in technology. 'We found that a great partnership was created through a great human relationship, between McLaren, between Mercedes, between the Ilmor guys. If you have people who have a great relationship but no technical depth, that does not help a lot. But if you have that technical depth and also a great human feeling among the partners, this is probably one of the most important factors to win races.'

Ilmor Engineering

Building the Mercedes–Benz F1 engine that provides the horsepower that motivates the McLaren cars is the work of Ilmor Engineering. Paul Morgan, who provides the 'mor' in Ilmor, has a love of engines that began when he was a boy growing up in Brixworth, near Northampton. Paul was born into an engineering environment and was influenced by his father's business of manufacturing automotive components and also his hobby of restoring vintage cars.

From the age of 15, Paul began rebuilding ancient automobiles himself in his father's workshop. Among his restoration projects were a Talbot–Lago Grand Prix car and a Lagonda Rapide, both of which he raced in competition. When he graduated from university in 1970 with a degree in Mechanical Engineering he found employment with the racing engine specialist Cosworth Engineering, where he could indulge himself in his twin passions of engines and competition.

Racing engines are a way of life for Ilmor's Paul Morgan, who still marvels at the way they work when stretched to their limits in F1.

To Paul Morgan engines can be not only efficient lumps of anonymous metal but also works of art, with personalities. His office at Ilmor is decorated with photos and drawings of the important engines in his life. He flies vintage aircraft as a hobby, including a Second World War Mustang fighter plane which has a 1650hp Rolls–Royce Merlin V12 engine. At home in his living room he has a spare example of that engine standing in the corner, like a piece of sculpture. Yet his business requires combining the aesthetics of form with the practicality of function, a reality that is nowhere more acutely reflected than in an engine stretched to its limits for F1 racing. And Paul Morgan still marvels at that.

'One of the things that always surprises us, though we work with it every day, is the speed at which the engine actually operates. Our engines are running well over 16,000rpm and therefore the pistons are going up and down something like 150 times a second. And to be able to suck air into the cylinder, set it on fire and expel it out through the exhaust port at that sort of speed takes a fair bit of believing that it can actually happen.'

teamwork · **the engine**

The tiny jewel-like 2998cc Mercedes–Benz F1 engine is made from nearly 6000 different components. Crafted from steel, aluminium alloy, titanium and other exotic metals the components are packaged in a compact unit, 590mm long, 500mm wide and 483mm high and weighing little more than 100kg. The crankshaft whirling around more than 16,000 times per minute thrusting each piston up and down in its cylinder at a rate of 150 times per second subjects the piston to forces 8500 times its own weight. The movement of the piston that rotates the camshaft, (there are four camshafts, two per bank of five cylinders) that opens and closes the four valves in each cylinder head is measured in milliseconds (1000 of which are contained in each second). Every revolution in each cylinder takes about 4 milliseconds.

During the firing phase, when the compressed mixture of air and fuel is ignited by a spark plug, the resultant explosion in the combustion chamber of the cylinder creates temperatures in excess of 2000 degrees centigrade. Small wonder then, when its components are subjected to such stresses and this process is multiplied by 10 cylinders, that the Mercedes F1 engine at speed sounds like a banshee gone berserk.

The tiny jewel-like Mercedes–Benz V10 F1 engine produces power, and noise, out of all proportion to its size. Small wonder then, that at speed it is often sounds like a banshee gone berserk.

"Although Ilmor is a business, it's run like a racing team."
Tyler Alexander

Many years ago, in the streets of the town of Chur in Switzerland, the much more subdued sounds coming out the exhaust pipes of passing saloon cars captured the imagination of a little boy named Mario Illien, whose parents never owned a car. Before long, by listening intently with his eyes closed, Mario could distinguish the exhaust notes made by different makes of cars and eventually he could even differentiate between models made by the same manufacturer.

Today, while standing at the pit wall at race tracks around the world, Mario Illien's finely tuned hearing can immediately detect the identity of a passing F1 car from its screaming exhaust note. For Mario no car sounds sweeter than a McLaren, the one with the Mercedes–Benz V10 in the back, the engine he designed.

Early in his life, the boy who listened to passing cars in Switzerland resolved to find a career that would enable him to become intimately involved with the magic forces of the internal combustion engine – particularly those used for racing, the highest expression of the art. Mario was fascinated by the technical descriptions of the engines he read about in racing magazines brought home by his brother, a motorsport enthusiast.

He watched F1 racing on television, and as a spectator at hillclimb events in Switzerland, where racing is banned, the sounds of the cars sent him into raptures. As a youth he found spare-time employment with a Swiss engine-builder and he also worked for a while as a mechanic for Jo Bonnier, the Swiss-based Swedish driver who was killed at Le Mans in 1972.

Before he went to university, Mario designed an engine for Formula 2 racing and another for motorcycle sidecar competition. In 1976, after getting his degree in Mechanical Engineering, Mario's first project was to design a solar heating system for his parent's house. In 1979, after a term as a designer of diesel engines for a Swiss manufacturer, his urge to create engines for racing inspired him to move to England, where he joined Cosworth Engineering. There, he worked with Paul Morgan and in 1984 they went out on their own, joining forces and their names to establish Ilmor Engineering in Brixworth.

right: **The screaming exhaust note of the engine is music to the ears of Mario Illien, the design genius responsible for creating it.**

teamwork · **the engine**

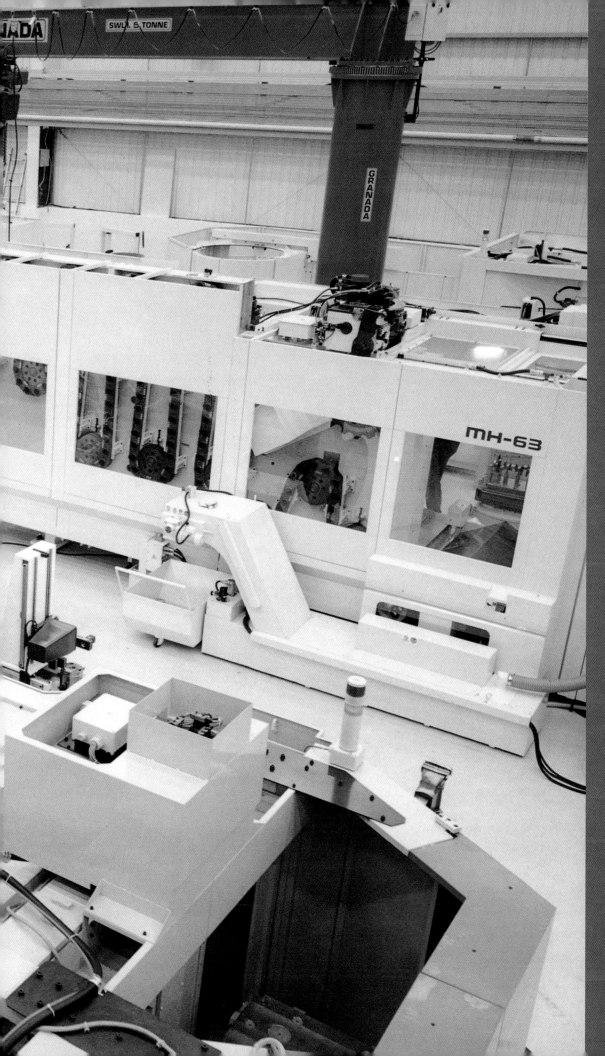

Among the hardest workers at Ilmor are the numerically controlled mechanical robots used to manufacture 98 per cent of all the components used by the company...

'Our pockets were empty, but our heads were full of ideas,' Mario remembers of those early days when they first set up shop in Paul Morgan's house. 'All we needed was a customer.' The knight-in-shining-armour of a customer took the form of the American IndyCar team entrant, Roger Penske. A shrewd and successful businessman, as well as a former racing driver, it took Penske only a brief audience with Illien and Morgan to become a believer in their vision. He became a 50 per cent shareholder in the budding Ilmor enterprise and a year later arranged for Chevrolet to take half his share, a quarter interest in the company, in exchange for Ilmor developing a Chevrolet-badged IndyCar engine, initially for the Penske team.

With funding from the automotive giant, the Chevrolet V8 was a roaring success, regularly winning IndyCar championships and, in 1991, powering the winning cars in all 17 races in the American-based series. Ilmor also supplied engines to several F1 teams, beginning in 1989, though the company's involvement at the pinnacle of motorsport remained sporadic due to budget constraints. In 1993, after 86 IndyCar race wins, Chevrolet ended its 10-year agreement with Ilmor and Mercedes–Benz took its place. When this partnership was equally and immediately successful, with the Mercedes engine winning the prestigious Indianapolis 500 event in its race debut, the links were forged that in 1994 were extended to include the Mercedes return to F1 racing.

For the 1995 season, when Mercedes and McLaren would put their new partnership to the Grand Prix test, the first completely new engine especially built to suit the McLaren chassis was fired up at Brixworth on 16 January at 4.35 in the afternoon. It was christened the Mercedes–Benz FO110 – 'FO' for Formula One, '1' for the first in the series and '10' for the number of cylinders. For Mario Illien it was a emotional moment – only 19 short weeks after he first sketched out the details of his 'baby'. His eyes glisten at recalling that 'incredibly intense, exciting and thoughtful moment'.

'There was obviously quite a bit of tension, especially since the first race was only a few weeks away. If there was a major problem we might have run out of time to solve it. And standing there, just before pressing the starter button, there was a prickly feeling.

Then it sprung into life and everybody was very happy. The whole factory was there and we sipped champagne. Today, that is still quite an exciting moment to remember.'

Paul Morgan, who is responsible for the manufacture of the engines his partner designs, thinks Mario's talent is rare. 'He's got a tremendous flair for designing motor racing engines. And he approaches the whole engine as a single concept, so you haven't got brackets and wires and pipes hanging all over the place. It's nicely neat and tidy, which is good from an aesthetic standpoint.'

Though Mario delights in the exotic sounds made by his creations he doesn't necessarily see them as works of art. He appreciates them more as 'harmonious objects'. An engine might also be an attractive arrangement of 6000 pieces of metal but his affection for it is only temporary. 'The problem I have when I look at an engine I designed, say, two or three years ago, is that it seems obsolete now. Almost like old junk. I sometimes wonder how I could have done it that way. It's not something I cherish, because it's something from the past.'

The relentless pace of F1 engine development, where today is already yesterday's tomorrow, leaves little time for nostalgia or sentiment for those at the forefront of the continual quest for improvement. One thing Mario does look back on fondly is the creative process, which in his case once meant marathon sessions at the drawing board wherein he would lock himself away from all distractions and work for 16 to 18 hours a day, seven days a week. He did this in his office at home, where his intense concentration was only interrupted by occasional taps on the door when his wife brought him food.

The relentless pace of engine development keeps over 300 Ilmor employees on the go, around the clock, throughout the year.

Nowadays, though he is still responsible for creating the original concepts, Mario spends more time presiding over the efforts of his select team of designers. The F1 project manager is Simon Armstrong, Stuart Grove is in charge of design detail and Max de Novellis looks after development. Including the group handling IndyCar projects there are nearly 50 people involved in engine design and development at

Ilmor, all especially selected for their capability to perform to their maximum under the pressure of limited time. To assess their potential, prospective employees are given a test, devised by Mario and reminiscent of the way he once spent those many solitary hours on his drawing board at home. Mario puts the candidates alone in a room, provides them with a pencil and paper, and asks them to design an engine component that has to fit into a given assembly. They've got half a day to come up with a solution.

With the computer-controlled dyno, engines are subjected to full Grand Prix race distances... and the results analysed to improve engine response, torque performance and fuel consumption.

'Technical qualifications are a good baseline,' says Mario of what it takes for him to hire an engine designer, 'but in discussion with somebody I find it difficult to assess what they are truly capable of doing. You can do all the studies at school but you also need flair and intuition. Our test helps evaluate how they can perform here. It is important that we pick people who love to compete, have a lot of self-motivation and can think for themselves.'

Yet these people also have to work together, like the individual components that must fit harmoniously into a given engine assembly. Taking on the Mercedes F1 project in 1993 meant the company had to double its workforce over a period of about 18 months. 'The good news,' according to Paul Morgan, 'was that when Mercedes joined us they were serious about their F1 racing and could provide the budget to produce a fairly healthy development programme. The more difficult news was that they wanted it right now.'

In the face of such rapid expansion there was a pressing need to introduce new recruits into the system and to each other, and, to make them feel at home, organize everyone into a united effort while maintaining the highest levels – and standards – of production. Among the hardest workers at Ilmor are the numerically controlled mechanical robots used to manufacture 98 per cent of all the components used by the company, and the machinery grinds away 24 hours a day, seven days a week. But the strength of the company rests with the human side of the operation. And, as Paul Morgan notes, 'It's much more difficult to get a good group of people working well together as a team than it is to get a group of machines up to speed.'

Fitting the over 300 employees (319 at the start of the 1998 season) into the scheme of things at Ilmor requires a carefully co-ordinated effort for them to become efficient cogs in the wheel. To help foster team spirit, as well as to perform the practical function of putting names to new faces, photographs of the personnel, with their names beneath them, are posted on the notice-board at the entrance to each department in the factory. Each department operates like an individual team and the notice-board also has on it a forecast of the production goals for the month. In this way everyone knows where they stand every day, which in this business is invariably under the starting gun of a race against time.

Another vital part of the Ilmor team is based at Stuttgart-Unterturkheim, where Mercedes engineers and technicians put the Brixworth-produced engines through their paces on a transient dynamometer. With the computer-controlled dyno, engines are subjected to full Grand Prix race distances – including gearchanges, braking and accelerating – and the results analysed to improve engine response, torque performance and fuel consumption. Also working with Ilmor in Germany is Dasa, the space research company of Daimler–Benz, which tests and experiments with new materials that might be used in racing engine construction. The close interaction between Mercedes and Ilmor includes exchanges of personnel as well as data.

Just as it is with Mercedes, the element of competition is a cornerstone of the Ilmor philosophy. Says Mario Illien: 'Either a person is a racer – has a competitive mind – or they are not. Designing and building racing engines is a challenge to compete and the fact that you get instant feedback at the races keeps you on your toes. You find out immediately if you have done a good or bad job. That helps to motivate everybody.'

"After each race we get the whole group together and tell them about the weekend. It was quite amazing after we won that first race in Australia in 1997. We opened a few bottles of champagne and you could see in everybody's faces that something very special had happened. It was a precious moment."
Mario Illien

Mark Grey, Tim White, Mario and John Coleman are, like all the people behind the Mercedes engines, racing enthusiasts.

the partners

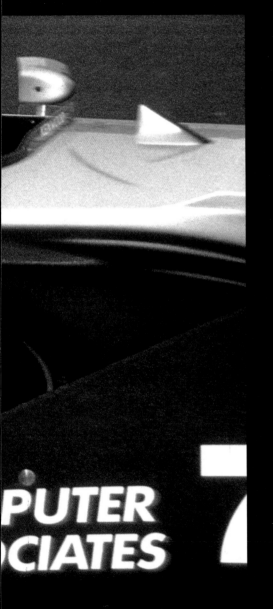

"Their track record alone would be enough to justify our investment, but when we spoke to Ron Dennis he explained to us not just McLaren's plans to build upon their on-track success but also the innovative and dynamic marketing and imaging programme that they had developed. We were even more convinced and excited about the possibilities."

LUDGER STABY
Spokesperson of the Board of Reemtsma

For the team's partners, F1 racing gives unparalleled exposure to a vast global audience.

exposure

F1 is many things to many people. To its fans it's a sport. To the teams it's a technical competition. To those who run it F1 is a business. But to those who pay for it, the investors who provide the vast amount of funding on which the most expensive sport in the world depends, F1 is a promotional vehicle providing exposure to an enormous global audience.

According to figures released by the Fédération Internationale de l'Automobile (FIA), the sport's governing body, a total of 50,732,645,052 viewers watched F1 on television in 1997. This cumulative F1 audience is based on telecasts of Grand Prix races, qualifying sessions, feature programmes and news coverage in over 200 countries. When radio broadcasts and print media coverage in newspapers (over 100 in Europe alone) and magazines are factored in, F1 spans the world as an annual sporting spectacle like no other. Only the Olympic Games and World Cup Soccer rival F1 audience figures, but these sporting events occur only once every four years, while F1 takes place over nine months of every year, giving ongoing and repeated exposure to a vast market of potential consumers.

For F1 to be used as an effective marketing tool, it requires much more than simply slapping a company name on the side of a high-speed billboard or on a famous driver's suit and helmet. The car and driver must be part of a team that can be competitive, since the level of exposure escalates dramatically with the position of the car in the running order in a race. Television cameras, especially, focus on the front-runners and when it comes to maximum exposure, the winner takes all. When it comes to winning F1 races McLaren has done it more than most. But the team's services to its investors do not end with the ceremony on the victory podium at a Grand Prix.

As Peter Stayner, head of Partner Management in TAG McLaren Marketing Services, explains: 'We don't just take the money and run. We establish the aims and objectives of our partners, then make sure their Formula 1 involvement works for them. Every company has got very specific goals. West, for instance, because of the rules against cigarette advertising in many areas, is mainly interested in the international exposure Formula 1 gives it, particularly on television. Boss, on the other hand, wants to be associated with the competitive image of Formula 1 and project this image into its retail clothing business to improve sales. Mobil, which supplies McLaren with fuel and lubricants, uses Formula 1 as a laboratory to improve its products and, more importantly, it uses the image of winning Formula 1 races as part of its marketing plan throughout the world. It's the same with all our partners.'

Peter notes that McLaren's partners fall into two main categories: commercial and technical – partnerships which are led, respectively, by West and Mercedes. Their identities are featured most prominently on the team's livery, which also includes an array of corporate partners and official suppliers. In all there are over two dozen corporate identities associated with the team, representing a diversified group of companies that provides a wide assortment of goods and services.

F1 is a promotional vehicle providing exposure to an enormous global audience.

West

In 1997 the team became known as West McLaren Mercedes when Reemtsma, one of Europe's leading tobacco manufacturers, was appointed McLaren's title partner through its most successful brand: West. Founded in 1910, with headquarters in Hamburg, Germany, Reemtsma brands (which also include Davidoff and Peter Stuyvesant) are sold in over 100 countries. It was in the interest of further expanding its markets that Reemtsma became associated with McLaren.

When announcing West's new F1 venture Ludger Staby, chairman of Reemtsma, explained why the company chose McLaren. 'To achieve our goals of enhanced global growth it was essential that we acquire a suitably high profile opportunity commensurate with our ambitions. When we first analysed the opportunities that might be available we never dreamed that our search would be ultimately so successful as to acquire the title rights to one of the giants of world sport, McLaren. Their track record alone would be enough to justify our investment, but when we spoke to Ron Dennis he explained to us not just McLaren's plans to build upon their on-track success but also the innovative and dynamic marketing and imaging programme that they had developed. We were even more convinced and excited about the possibilities.'

Dieter Weng, a member of Reemtsma's management board and responsible for the company's marketing issues, notes that for marketing on a global scale there are only three events to consider. 'It's either the Olympics, the World Cup Football Championship or Formula 1. While the first two occur basically every four years, the latter happens all the time, 16 or 17 times a year. In Formula 1 the audience accumulates over the year to a much bigger number and you therefore have a continuous impact. Every Grand Prix has enormous energy. It's a huge crowd-gathering sports event, with a lot of elements in it that are invigorating and involving people's minds and emotions.'

West's Dieter Weng (with Ron Dennis) notes that every Grand Prix has an enormous energy that involves people's minds and emotions.

Dieter was directly involved with TAG McLaren Marketing Services and the several design firms charged with merging West's identity with those of McLaren and Mercedes. The goal was to establish a synergy between the companies by adding visual elements of West's image and 'use the team as a turbo-charger'. Besides the West logo, with its 'rocket red' and black slashes, a main feature of a West cigarette package that also appears on the McLaren livery is the 'Mirror Man', a red and black graphic design device that is intended to communicate an attitude to life. 'What it suggests,' Dieter says, 'is "Go through your life not one-dimensionally, but open doors, look at things, and once you look at things, you will find them looking quite differently as well." '

When applying this investigative philosophy to West's F1 partner, Dieter Weng has discovered what he thinks is the essence of McLaren's 'personality'. 'It is a pretty unique combination of technology, precision and logic. It is very down to earth, but also very active and has a youthfulness that is quite different from other teams. Through its individuals it has a wide variety of aspects and attitudes, including self-awareness and self-esteem, which you need to compete successfully at such a high level. Everything about McLaren starts at the top. In Ron Dennis I've rarely met anyone who has such a clear picture about where he wants to carry things. He's very goal-oriented and very creative, and makes an extreme effort to think things through to achieve those goals.'

technology partners

McLaren's Mercedes engine has over 900 moving parts; some of them move at over 370 kilometres per hour, a speed that generates such friction that some internal surfaces reach a temperature of more than 300 degrees centigrade during a typical Grand Prix, when the engine will complete more than a million revolutions. The important task of lubricating these mechanical extremes – and supplying the fuel on which the engine runs, as well as the grease and hydraulic fluids for the car's moving parts – is entrusted to the team's technology partner, Mobil.

Mobil – with activities in the exploration and production of crude oil and natural gas, refining, marketing, petrochemicals, mining and minerals, real estate and research – is one of the largest industrial companies in the world, doing business in over 125 countries and employing over 40,000 people. It is also one of the oldest industrial companies, originating over a century ago, and supplying fuel and lubricants for such historic events as the 1909 world automobile speed record of 205kph set by a Mobil-lubricated Benz, the Wright brothers' early flights and Charles Lindbergh's transatlantic crossing in 1927. After pioneering the development of synthetic oils for jet aircraft engines, Mobil introduced the first fully synthetic automotive engine oil in 1973. Involved in F1 racing since 1978, and with McLaren since 28 October 1994, Mobil has over 50 Grand Prix wins to its credit.

Mobil's man at the races, and an employee for over a quarter of a century, is Tony Harlow, the company's motorsport technical co-ordinator. 'I'm responsible for co-ordinating all the technical development programmes on fuels, lubricants and greases to support our Formula 1 activity – including all the logistics associated with blending the fuels and lubricants, and getting them appropriately distributed to the tests, as well as the races.'

Most of the technology partners supply McLaren with their products, including computer-related companies, all of which are world leaders in their fields.

Tony notes that for Mobil, a West McLaren Mercedes F1 car acts not only as a promotional vehicle but also as a chemical laboratory in which to perfect its products. And, despite the exotic use to which it is put in the Mercedes F1 engine, Mobil 1 fuel could also be used in road cars. 'The regulations are such that the fuel we use is very close to ordinary pump fuel. We use the same components. The difference is in the relative proportions of the individual components. By blending them differently the mixture is optimized for the higher-revving requirements of Formula 1, but even so, it would be suitable for the average road car. As it is with the McLaren car and the Mercedes engine, we have a continuous development programme with constant revisions made to match the specific demands as they evolve.'

Tony Harlow is Mobil's man at the races. His company uses its involvement with the team as both a promotional vehicle and a chemical laboratory.

Most of the technology partners supply McLaren with their products, including computer-related companies, all of which are world leaders in their fields. Computer Associates is a supplier of mission-critical computer software for business applications. Sun Microsystems supplies Unix-based distributed networked computer servers (including over 60 percent of the servers that hold the pages on the World Wide Web) and workstation systems. PTC/Computervision Parametric Technology Corporation is a supplier of CAD/CAM/CAE and PDM software. SAP is a leader in client/server standard business application software. Cadence supplies electronic design animation offering technology and services to accelerate design and performance in electronics. And Kenwood – an international leader in home and car audio equipment – supplies the radio communications equipment for the Race Team.

Another technology partner is British Aerospace (Europe's leading aerospace and defence company), and a recently acquired partner is Siemens AG – one of the most respected international companies in the development, manufacture and marketing of electronics, telecommunications and electrical engineering. Siemens operates in over 190 countries and employs 386,000 people.

Besides having its identity on the McLaren cars, Loctite – supplier of proprietary high-performance adhesives, sealants and specialized brand name chemicals – supplies the glue (eight different types of adhesive) that literally hold the McLaren cars and the Mercedes engines together.

official suppliers

In 1998, following Goodyear's decision to leave F1 at the end of the season, the West McLaren Mercedes team began using tyres supplied by Bridgestone – one of the largest manufacturers of tyres and rubber products – which entered F1 competition in 1997. Hiroshi Yasukawa, Bridgestone's Motorsports director, explains why the Japanese-based company, which has operations around the world, chose to go with McLaren and how the partnership paid off immediately, giving Bridgestone its first F1 victory in its very first race with the team.

Bridgestone's partnership with West McLaren Mercedes began with its first F1 victory in its very first appearance with the team.

'We worked with four very good F1 teams during 1997, but McLaren operates at a higher level and also displays a very methodical and disciplined approach. This enabled our research and development departments to work together and achieve very significant progress. Our partnership with McLaren puts very big pressure on us, but we regard this as very good and positive for our activities. All our staff are extremely happy to have the opportunity to work with the McLaren team and with Mercedes–Benz.'

"Many companies have vision statements, and ours is to win every Grand Prix. If we don't win every Grand Prix then we are not fulfilling our objective – for ourselves and for our partners."
Ron Dennis

The Bridgestone tyres on the McLarens are mounted on Enkei wheels, the suspension springs are supplied by Eibach, and GS Batteries are also used in the cars. In the pit garages at Grand Prix circuits the team benefits from the work of Targetti – suppliers of lighting appliances – which developed the lighting system for the overhead modules used to provide all the services to the race cars. At McLaren's headquarters in Woking, Targetti additionally helped develop a sophisticated new lighting system for the executive dining room, reception and trophy room. Also at the factory where the cars are built, extensive use is made of electro discharge machinery (EDM) provided by Charmilles Technologies. On the factory floor, in the design offices and in the garages at the races the team uses Samsung/AST monitors and PCs. Another official supplier, Sports Marketing Surveys, provides the data and statistics that help keep McLaren's marketing effort on course.

corporate partners

Among the team's corporate partners is Hugo Boss – supplier of the team's clothing and, operating in 75 countries, a world leader in men's fashion. Another partner is TAG Heuer (part of the TAG Group of which McLaren International is also a member company), makers of high-quality Swiss sports watches and also the official F1 timekeeper since 1992. Another corporate partner is Camozzi – leading suppliers of pneumatic systems for factory automation. Beverage companies represented among the corporate partners are Schweppes (an internationally recognized leading brand of mixers and soft drinks), Finlandia (a leading premium brand of vodka) and Warsteiner (the top brand of premium German Pils beer).

left: **Over two dozen corporate identities representing a diversified group of international companies are associated with the team.**

the race team

"They are the most human team. From the outside there might be a different perception, but it's true."

ALAIN PROST
(former McLaren driver and now a team owner)

testing

McLaren does more testing than racing. Test programmes, devised back at the factory by Chief Designer Neil Oatley, are conducted according to a strict procedure based on his job list. The essential goal of testing is to improve the performance and reliability of the race equipment – a lengthy and exacting process that can be something of an endurance test for the personnel who are involved.

The team does more testing than racing. The long hours necessary to improve reliability and performance can be an endurance test for the personnel.

A typical test day begins at nine in the morning and continues until six in the evening, interrupted only by a short break for lunch provided by the catering staff who accompany the team. Changing engines and gearboxes, preparing new set-ups for the next day and so on, can extend working hours until midnight or beyond. Most tests continue for four or five days and test sessions are conducted nearly every second week throughout the year.

However, as Technical Director Adrian Newey explains: 'The more testing you do doesn't necessarily mean the better you'll be. Much depends on how the tests are structured. If you're only turning up at a test and bashing around madly to see what happens, nothing much happens. You have to set specific goals and targets, and pursue them diligently. What we do at each test is to carry out what is essentially a collation of a lot of ideas from our design people at the factory.'

While Steve Nichols is now factory-based as Head of Future Projects, he is highly respected as a developmental engineer and, over the course of his lengthy F1 career, has spent countless hours at test sessions.

'If your test is badly planned and organized, and you're doing the wrong things, it can be a complete waste of time. I always try to remember the purpose of each test session. You're trying to learn as much as possible and the best way to do that is to

start from the outside and work in. You start with what I call "coarse work", a radical set-up change to the chassis, for instance. You try it for a few laps, bring the car in, get the driver's feedback, check the telemetry results and the data logging printouts, make another change, do some more laps, check it out again and so on. In this way you can zero in on the details necessary for continual improvement until you reach the optimum chassis setting. When this is done satisfactorily in testing you're only left with fine tuning when you go racing.'

Nichols feels that, 'you need a different mind-set for testing than racing. A race weekend is much more intense; there's only a very limited time to get everything right and a need for instant solutions. Some people try to run a test the same way, but it doesn't work and it isn't necessary. You have much more time in a test and you must use it, by being calm and methodical. Some people just can't respond to the way you have to think at tests and they get bored.'

Testing times for Del Jeanes (veteran truckie) and Adrian Newey. Sessions are structured with specific goals and targets that are pursued diligently.

the test team

The Test Team is considered to be part of the Race Team, which it closely resembles. When, in 1987, McLaren first established a team dedicated to testing, the idea was to replicate the Race Team, yet operate independently from it. Prior to this, testing was conducted on a more informal basis, with personnel and equipment from the Race Team.

"The impression down the pit lane was that McLaren had the best equipment, the best image and they were also the best to their employees."

The task of organizing and managing the Test Team was given to one of McLaren's longer-serving employees, Indy Lall. Besides testing the cars, Indy's team is also a training ground for personnel who can gain experience without the pressure of working under race conditions. Though there is a regular turnover of people who later move on to other jobs within McLaren, and senior members of the Race Team also often attend tests, several veteran members form the backbone of the approximately 20 people in the Test Team.

Engineering on the cars – two of them at most test sessions – is the responsibility of Mark Williams, the engineer/co-ordinator, who also normally uses engineers from the Race Team with him to run the cars. Chief Mechanic Ian Dyer presides over seven mechanics, three on each car and one 'floating' who applies his spanners where required. There are two gearbox technicians and another man responsible for engine preparation. The four truckies, besides driving the two Test Team transporters to the circuits, also look after the wheels, tyres and spares and one of them performs timing duties. Another important task of the truckies is to monitor the mileage of every single component, as part of the 'lifing' procedure. Though it is run like the Race Team, the Test Team has a life of its own.

Roy Reader, a truckie, first joined McLaren in 1970 and was a member of the Race Team for 14 years. Then, tired of all the travelling and wanting to spend more time with his family, Roy ran a guest house for seven years. But as several others have done, he came back.

right: **The Test Team closely resembles the Race Team, yet operates independently from it and has a life of its own.**

'I always stayed in touch and was made more than welcome to pop into the factory, look around and talk to the guys. There's a tremendous loyalty here; you'll find that

even when people leave for a while, a lot of them come back. That's a good thing and I think the company appreciates it as well. Having started very early at McLaren, when it was still like a family run business, I have this sense that it's still got its roots and you feel you're still part of the family.'

Barry Ultahan, a gearbox technician, became a member of the McLaren family in 1983, and is an official member of The Wrinklies. One main reason for his longevity and loyalty to the team is his high regard for the head of the family.

'Ron is a superb boss to work for,' says Barry. 'He really cares about people and if you have any personal problems he will do his best to sort them out for you. He's helped a lot of us that way in the past. Of course, he's very demanding. He has to be to get the kind of superiority that McLaren holds over near enough every team down the pit lane.'

Barry has been around long enough to know what's expected of the employees, but when newcomers come to the Test Team it is part of Indy Lall's job to teach them the McLaren way of working.

There are approximately 20 people in the Test Team, which also functions as a kind of school for newcomers.

'You bring them on, you encourage them, you demonstrate, you explain, you show them the rights and wrongs,' says Indy, the patient schoolmaster. 'We don't leave any stone unturned. Safety is of the utmost importance. There are precise procedures in every aspect of McLaren that have to be adhered to every step of the way. You encourage people to play a part. The more you are involved, the more feedback you get yourself and the more you enjoy your job. That philosophy goes through the entire workforce.'

Ian Dyer, the chief mechanic and a member of the McLaren workforce for over a dozen years, notes how that philosophy provokes admiration from visitors when they see the Test Team at work. 'They're mightily impressed. The presentation of the cars, the clothing we wear, the partitions in the garage, how clean and neat and tidy and well organized it all is – I think that's what everybody is amazed at.'

Paul Wallace recently joined the Test Team as a senior mechanic, after spending a few months with another F1 team. According to Paul, 'The impression down the pit lane was that McLaren had the best equipment, the best image and they were also the best to their employees. And that's the way I've found it to be. For sure, the people in charge want you to do your job 100 per cent, which is what any self-respecting mechanic wants to do.'

engine testing
Working in tandem with the McLaren Test Team are five people from Ilmor Engineering, whose job is to put the Mercedes V10 through its paces. The permanent members include Test Engineer Robin Page, another engineer, an engine builder and a truckie. Accompanying them is one other Ilmor employee, a different one each time, who gets the opportunity to see the engines in action.

Robin Page, an Ilmor employee since he left school in 1990, became intimately acquainted with engines long before that. At the age of 11 he rebuilt the engine of his motorbike, and when studying for his degree in Mechanical Engineering it was always his intention to put his professional credentials to the test in competition.

'I think there is a danger that if you work in other branches of engineering you will become very specialized, with a narrow focus, and become frustrated by working on long-term projects. In racing, it's much more immediate and you have a chance to be more creative. You can conceive an idea, execute it, test it and get the result in a very short time frame.'

And when it comes to going testing as opposed to racing, Robin thinks the former pursuit has an edge for engine men who particularly enjoy the experimental aspect of their job.

'At a Grand Prix, running is quite restricted before the race itself, so it's difficult to change very much. The guys on the Race Team are locked into one spec of an engine and, really, you can end up as passengers that way. At a test we get to try new tweaks, and that can be very stimulating,' he says.

test driving
Both Mika Hakkinen and David Coulthard have plenty of experience testing. Mika started at McLaren as a test driver before he became part of the Race Team, and David began his F1 career as a test driver with Williams.

"You cannot rest on your laurels. That is the one basic lesson you learn in this business. It's one thing getting up there. It's another sustaining it. Testing is an important part of this process."
Indy Lall

For a test driver, consistency is as important as speed. He must lap quickly enough to simulate race conditions, while maintaining that pace as evenly as possible so as to provide a steady platform on which the performance of the car and engine can be best evaluated. The test driver's pace must be accompanied by a sensitivity and feel for the car's behaviour, and he must have enough technical understanding and the necessary powers of observation to be able to relate detailed information to the engineers. Some so-called 'natural' racing drivers aren't that good as test drivers because they instinctively compensate for any problems in the car. They simply drive around the difficulties and are unable to provide any relevant feedback to make improvements.

Testing is no problem for Mika, says Test Team Manager Indy Lall, because, 'he eats, drinks and sleeps motor racing, even when he's off duty. He always wants things to happen as quickly as possible, so for him testing is almost as good as racing.'

David particularly enjoys testing new parts. 'Bolt-on bits, something I can pick up and look at and think, "Right, this is what the designer has come up with; we'll put this on the car and see what it's going to do." That really excites me more than trying different mixtures on the engine, or software and the like. I don't mind endurance runs either because you can experiment with driving, learning about different lines and so on, which you can't do on three- or four-lap runs. To a certain extent testing also helps a driver, by keeping you in trim between races.'

the race team

Nearly every second weekend for nine months of the year the Race Team is at another Grand Prix. On average, 60 people attend each race as part of the West McLaren Mercedes team. Leading the entourage are Ron Dennis (Team Principal), Norbert Haug (Head of Mercedes–Benz Motorsport), Mario Illien (the engine designer), Adrian Newey (the team's Technical Director), Dave Ryan (Race Team Manager) and Jo Ramirez (Team Co-ordinator).

The Race Team personnel who look after Mika Hakkinen's and David Coulthard's cars are headed by Steve Hallam, head of Race Engineering and Mike Negline, chief mechanic. Each of the two cars has three engineers (a race engineer in charge of the car, an embedded systems engineer and a data analyst engineer) and three mechanics (a senior or Number One mechanic and two second or Number Two mechanics). Three other mechanics are responsible for the spare car. There are three gearbox

Ron, Adrian, Norbert and Mario (l–r) on the pit lane timing stand where they observe and direct the team's operations on race weekends.

technicians (one per car) two data analysis technicians and one fabricator. There are also eight engine support personnel, seven truckies, two physiotherapists (one per driver), two Kenwood radio engineers, two Bridgestone Tyre engineers and a Mobil fuel and lubricant specialist. Also on hand are several marketing co-ordinators, two press officers (from McLaren and Mercedes), the hospitality staff, the motorhome staff, representatives of the team's partners, and assorted guests.

home from home

Outside the garages the team's trucks are parked precisely, to the centimetre, using a measuring tape and a mathematical formula.

To each European Grand Prix the team brings two large McLaren trucks (one carrying three race cars, the other support equipment), a Mercedes/Ilmor truck (carrying up to 15 engines), a Mobil truck (carrying the fuel, the refuelling rigs and also the portable interior fittings and servicing equipment for the garages), three motorhomes (one each for West, McLaren and Mercedes) and support trucks for the motorhomes. There are also several minibuses and Mercedes cars for travel between the circuit and the hotel. For the 'flyaway' events outside Europe, the cars and equipment are transported by air and the personnel work out of the facilities available at the circuits. In each case, and usually on a Tuesday before the Sunday Grand Prix, the first order of business is to transform the allotted pit, garage and paddock spaces (which are usually already finished to a high standard) into a McLaren-style environment.

In the paddock and at the back of the garages the motorhomes and trucks (all powered by Mercedes–Benz) are parked to perfection (to the centimetre, using a measuring tape and a mathematical formula), and the pit and garage floors are carefully painted the requisite shade of grey. Erected at the pit wall are the two canopied timing stands (which some refer to irreverently as the 'Prat Perches') from where senior personnel will direct the race.

Above the race cars in the garages, the overhead lighting and electronic modules are suspended from the ceiling. Placed against the garage walls are the custom-made grey and silver aluminium-framed panels, which are tastefully decorated with graphic arrangements in black of the corporate logos of the team and its partners. Also brought in from the trucks and positioned precisely in the garage are the pristine Lista cabinets containing the mechanics' tools neatly arranged like surgical instruments, the monitors (or 'Battle Stations', as Tyler Alexander – one of the longest serving members of the team – calls them) on which the telemetry output is displayed the tower units containing the team's 60 headsets and so on.

In the garages, where the floors are freshly painted, the custom-made lighting and electronic modules are suspended from the ceiling.

Once their main cargo is distributed the trucks, now scrubbed and polished to a sparkling finish outside the back doors of the garages, act as extensions of the immaculate factory in Woking. Contained in the main body of the race truck, though carefully packed into compartments and out of sight, are a spare chassis and the main components necessary to rebuild the cars. At the back is a 'hideaway' office, where the data engineers confer and work on computer programming. The other truck (called the Lista because it carries the Swiss-styled, McLaren-made Lista cabinets) contains a full workshop, with a lathe, a machining mill and all necessary fabricating equipment, as well as spare brakes, gearboxes and so on. This truck also has a larder and two refrigerators (both filled with snacks and drinks) and storage lockers containing drivers' clothing.

motorhomes

Across the paddock from the trucks are the three motorhomes, which function as headquarters and meeting rooms for senior personnel, as well as conference and entertainment centres for visitors. Each motorhome has a canopy extension, beneath which tables and chairs are placed. It is here that media interviews are conducted and invited guests are wined and dined with food and refreshments served from the motorhome kitchens.

The Mercedes motorhome tends to be where the media congregates, while the West motorhome contains an office for the race engineers and also provides the 'sit-down' meals when the Race Team works late. The McLaren motorhome dominates the paddock and functions as the operational heart of the team at the races. A pet project of Ron Dennis, whose concept it was, the unique unit took two and a half years and a great deal of money to produce. Intended as a place where business can be done and partners looked after, Ron says it is 'not a motorhome, but a business tool', though most people refer to it as 'Ron's World'.

Across the paddock from the trucks are the three motorhomes, which function as headquarters and meeting rooms for senior personnel...

On the road, with the 14 metre long, three-axle trailer towed by a Mercedes–Benz Actros 571bhp tractor unit, the complete rig weighs 38 tonnes. Arriving at its designated parking space in the paddock, the tractor unit is taken elsewhere and the two-storey entirety of Ron's World comes majestically into being. At the touch of a button a computer-controlled hydraulic system levels and stabilizes the unit to within 5 millimetres over its full length. Another button is pressed and the entire top section of the trailer rises to its full height of 5 metres. From a special hatch in the roof the generator exhaust pipe and the satellite and TV antennae emerge; the satellite dish locks onto its pre-programmed host unit and communications are established to the team's radio networks at the circuit, to the factory back at Woking and to the world at large. More buttons are pushed – and some physical labour exerted – to erect the conservatory-style side extension, the floor of which weighs nearly 2 tonnes to insure maximum stability and keep Ron's World visitors high and dry in inclement weather.

The job of running this exclusive domain was entrusted to Shaune McMurray, a New Zealand native and a McLaren woman since 1977. Though curious sightseers throng around outside in the hope of getting a look inside, such visits are by invitation only. To those who make it across the threshold into the air-conditioned, sound-proofed, gadget-laden, leather-trimmed, luxuriously appointed, grey-hued edifice, Shaune is an enthusiastic tour guide.

'It's a fantastic place and easy to work in. There are essentially five areas inside. At the back on the lower floor is the drivers' room, where there are two fold-down benches for Mika and David to relax on, plus a massage table for the physiotherapists to work on them. As well as the treatment area, there are two separate TV, video and audio systems (one for each driver) and a large shower/steam room.

'Forward of the driver area is the lobby where there is an automatic lavatory. To the right, behind one of the air-operated doors, is the kitchen which has two freezers, two fridges, a dishwasher, gas cooker, microwave oven and a "dumb waiter" for delivering drinks and meals to the upper floor.

'To get to the upper floor there's a spiral aluminium staircase, which takes you into the central PA, secretarial and press officer area. At one end is Ron's office and at the other is a fully fitted presentation area with electrically operated seats and a viewing screen on which any combination of audio and visual presentations can be made. This room also has satellite decoders, a CD and mini-disc system, laser players, amplifiers and computer projection systems.'

Shaune confides that the complexity of the high-tech appointments once caught out the man after whom this 'World' is named. 'When it was still brand new Ron was showing Norbert Haug, from Mercedes, around and he accidentally dumped the air from the door operating system and locked them both in!'

"Anything that can improve the performance of the company, any opportunity that presents itself, then we are going to take that opportunity. If we can be better we will be better."
Ron Dennis

Heidi Wichlinski, DC's girlfriend, and Lisa Dennis, Ron's wife, enjoy the team's motorhome comforts.

The McLaren motorhome dominates the paddock and functions as the operational heart of the team at the races.

Shaune has many happy memories of her years as the motorhome 'Mum' to a succession of McLaren drivers. She remembers how fun-loving types like James Hunt and Gerhard Berger played practical jokes at her expense, and how Ayrton Senna used to come and visit her home in New Zealand. There, she acknowledges, the McMurray premises are kept neat and tidy, similar to the way things are kept in the McLaren paddocks around the world. Says Shaune: 'Everything has to reflect the McLaren way of doing things. The best way to describe that is that everything is as perfect as it can be.'

Early in 1998, Shaune decided that after over two decades of travelling with the team she would like to spend more time at the 10-acre McMurray farm in New Zealand, looking after the cattle, chickens, dogs and cats. But the McMurray clan is still represented at the races by Shaune's husband Bob, and also by their nephew on the Test Team, Rhodri Griffiths. At the races, Bob McMurray is in charge of the three motorhomes and also looks after the team's VIP Club in the paddock.

Mansour and Ron with Michael Douglas, movie star and a friend of the team.

the VIP club

Setting up the custom-made VIP hospitality suite is a laborious process. Like the rest of McLaren's race-going equipment the VIP area is an extension of headquarters – and no expense is spared in pursuing its perfection. Introduced in 1989, it has been expanding ever since and can now accommodate up to 1200 guests on a Grand Prix weekend. Depending on the venue, the stylish and lavish club environment is either tent-based or contained in the circuit's F1 Paddock Club area. The interior, decorated in the team livery, features wood-panelled walls, leather sofas and carpeting throughout. There is a separate bistro-style dining area, a bar and a lounge, with banks of TV screens, timing monitors and audio links so guests can watch the track action.

'This is a million dollar interior,' says Bob McMurray. 'It's not just a question of putting up a few pictures and scattering a few plants around. The suite comes to all the races, except the "flyaways", where certain elements of it are used. It grows or contracts according to the number of guests we have. There is even a double-decker, two-storey version that we bring to some races. We have a company that comes and fits it together for us. When we have the full-size unit it takes four or five guys four days to set it up and "McLarenize" it completely.'

Once the VIP Club has been fully McLarenized to Bob's satisfaction, personnel from TAG McLaren Marketing Services use the facility to entertain the team's guests. Head of VIP Hospitality is Caroline Sayers who, along with Peter Burns, head of Client Services, helped develop and upgrade the Club concept.

'Before we took the decision to do our own thing,' Caroline notes, 'hospitality meant a marquee in a tented village, dressed with garden furniture and some potted plants. There was nothing to distinguish one team's facilities from another's.

Mika with German Chancellor Helmut Kohl (*top*) **and David with tennis star Boris Becker** (*bottom*).

'Now, our guests are amazed at how sumptuous the interior is. It has an air of permanency that one does not expect to find in this sort of facility. In addition to being entertained while enjoying the racing, sponsors and their guests use the facility as a business tool, networking with other partners and suppliers and making new contacts in a McLaren-style environment. Other teams have tried to copy elements of the McLaren package, but when it comes to a day at the races, nobody does it better.'

'It's the McLaren way of doing things,' according to Bob. 'With all the jobs I've been involved in over the years – and I've driven the trucks, worked on the cars, you name it, I've done it – the most important thing is to get it right and do the job in the most professional way. Take parking the motorhomes, for instance. We jockey them around until there is exactly 1 metre between them. We're dealing with millimetres here so we take longer to park than most people, but that's only because we're getting it perfect. It's part of looking right. Take the tables and chairs under the motorhome canopy. Their bases and the chair legs are lined up exactly on the same line. Everything has to be tidied up and shipshape. You know, in many ways the most satisfying part of my job is on a Thursday evening when everything that you have aimed at in the set-up is done and everything works. You can actually step back and say, "Well, that worked. That went right. We're looking good." '

catering

While Bob McMurray is busy pursuing perfection in the paddock, Lyndy Woodcock and her crew are making preparations to cook up a storm in the motorhomes, where they will serve up to 120 people a day.

Lyndy has a Cordon Blue diploma and has cooked for families in France, been a chef on a yacht cruising the Mediterranean and now operates Absolute Taste, her own catering company, which has become part of the TAG McLaren Group. She has been with McLaren since 1991 and looks after the food for both the Race and Test Teams. For Lyndy and the four people who help her at the track, the days are long – often from five in the morning until 10 at night – and they have to eat on the run. They arrive at the circuits on the Tuesday before a race and have to be fully

Lyndy Woodcock and Sasha Osbourne prepare and serve the finest cuisine, but seldom have time to sample it themselves.

operational by Thursday. From then on it's a steady diet of breakfasts, lunches and dinners, up to 400 meals every day.

'We do the shopping in the local supermarkets and always try to have some of the traditional cuisine from the country we're in. In Hungary we do goulash; in England we do poached salmon, with new potatoes and Hollandaise sauce; and we serve a lot of Italian-style pasta wherever we are. The mechanics have lunch in the garage and we serve them sandwiches, crudities and maybe pizza to keep them going. They have a full English breakfast in the motorhome. We bring sausages, bacon, baked beans, tomato sauce and the like from England. About half of the mechanics go for a full fry-up, but more and more we're giving them muesli and yoghurt. We're making the guys more nutritionally aware.

The catering personnel arrive at the circuits on the Tuesday before a race and have to be fully operational by Thursday. From then on it's a steady diet of breakfasts, lunches and dinners, up to 400 meals every day.

'For the VIP meals we do a full menu: salads, three main courses and three puddings. Everything is home-made and cooked to order, and we design the food on the plates. It's all fresh and picture-perfect. If we're serving meat, it will be placed on the right-hand side, with a potato at precisely nine o'clock, the beans at two o'clock and a garnish placed just so. And every plate arrangement has to be exactly the same.'

Things can get 'pretty manic' for Lyndy, but she loves her job and can always manage a smile as she scurries around her motorhome kitchen and the serving areas that look like fashionable restaurants.

'You know, McLaren is always one step ahead of the other teams and we try to show that in the food, the serving and the presentation. Ron wants the whole team to be the best and look the best, and that's why I like working here. We try to do the best food in the paddock, and the equipment we have to work with is sparkling and polished – lots of chrome and black and silver – and all very trendy. It's such a pleasure to work with beautiful things.'

the truckies

While the motorhomes are being brought up to speed in the paddock, another advance party is dashing to and fro in the garage area. This is the truckies, so-called because they drive the convoy of trucks to and from the circuits – though that task is only a small part of the work they do. Once their set-up duty is done the truckies become an integral part of the Race Team, where they assume a variety of roles.

Gerry Good and his fellow truckies spend many hours transforming a Grand Prix garage into a McLaren-style working environment.

The first truckies to arrive – usually on a Tuesday before race weekend at the European races – are Gerry Good and Steve Morrow, who drive the Mobil support truck which carries all the garage equipment. Their first job is to wash the garage floor, then paint it, leaving it to dry overnight. Then, it takes them from 12 to 14 hours to set up the timing stands on the pit wall, install the garage wall panels, the overhead modules, the telemetry monitors, the radio sets, the wiring, the air lines and so on. The garage set-up is usually finished by midday on Wednesday, when the other trucks arrive.

His fellow truckies say that Gerry 'Gez' Good, who has been with McLaren since 1988, is one of the hardest workers and also one of the happiest guys on the team. For Gez, it seems, the amount of work he has to do and the state of his mind are closely connected.

'Yeah,' he smiles, 'I like being busy most of the time. I hope they appreciate the two and half days it takes us to make the place look like the factory. When all that's done I'm the team first-aider as well. I take a course every three years. It's mostly cuts and bruises, a few burns, some insect stings that I have to deal with. Nothing drastic, fortunately. The other thing I do is handle the pit board for Mika during the race. When the cars go out on the grid, even after so many races, you still get the old butterflies in the stomach. It's quite exciting up there on the timing stand.'

Few have a more exciting race day job than Steve Morrow, known to his team-mates as 'Forklift' or 'Forks'. During pit stops, Forks is at the sharp end of the stick operating the fuel nozzle. His other main job is as tyre man, looking after the mount programme for both race cars and the tyre pressures for David Coulthard's car. Forks is a big strong man, though his nickname resulted from a misunderstanding concerning his strength. Soon after he started with McLaren, in 1984, 'the team manager saw me lifting an engine into the back of a van by myself. He said, "You're like a bloody forklift!" It was actually a dummy engine, so it wasn't particularly heavy, but the name stuck. You'll find most of the guys here have nicknames.

'There's a sense of humour that runs through the team all the time, which is a good constant. It starts with the people who have been at McLaren over quite a few years. There's a lot of loyalty and I think, in overall terms, the team has the best policy towards its staff. Salaries are very good and the bonus system is very good and fair, because it involves the people at the factory as well. They get a percentage based on the points we score throughout the season, which is a reflection of the work they put into the team, even though they're not actually at the circuit. So, it helps keep everybody feeling involved.

For Steve 'Forklift' Morrow and the other truckies, driving the trucks is only one of their many jobs.

'But it's not just the money. We're all here to win and the money is just a bonus. It's very difficult when you sort of drop off the pace. The mood goes down and the struggle to find those few tenths of second is very intense. But once you see the performance of the car improving and your position is moving up, it gives everybody a big lift. And when we're winning again everybody perks up.'

Steve Cook's title is chief truckie. However, since much of his body is covered with tattoos, he is known to one and all as 'Tats'. As head of the seven truckies, Tats supervizes their work and assigns

previous page: **A pit stop, involving some 20 people, epitomizes F1 teamwork.**

duties. He is also the ringleader when it comes to assigning nicknames to his mates. Officially, he is in charge of loading and unloading the trucks, setting up the garage and handling the tyres, with the particular responsibility of looking after the tyre pressures on Mika Hakkinen's car. Tats is also the unofficial chief truck-parker and has taken it upon himself to be the team's visual monitor. He takes his jobs seriously, but plays down the significance of his chief truckie title.

'We're all equal. It's like on the race cars, where the mechanics have a Number One to liaise with. It's just a case of someone being the spokesperson for the truckies. Collectively, with the other guys, we're responsible for doing the job. When people walk through the garage and you hear comments such as "It's like a hospital in here", it makes us feel like we've done our jobs.'

In his role as visual monitor, Tats is particularly pleased with such compliments. 'The thing is, it's my job to make sure the little things aren't missed. When you're on the Race Team, with Ron around, you've got to keep looking at everything, because he does the same thing. From some distance away he can spot a truck that is parked hardly half an inch out of line. It only happened once, in 1992 I think it was, and ever since then we've been measuring it. You see him walking around inspecting everything and if he doesn't say anything you know there is nothing wrong. If he's got some very important people coming in he'll tell us to take even more care, but we try to adopt that attitude all the time. We want to be recognized for professionalism.'

Tats started with McLaren in 1984 and after five years moved a little further along the pit lane to work with another team. There, it didn't take him long to find out he missed his former team, and the team missed him.

'Things weren't happening the way I liked, the way they do at McLaren, and I made some noises in that respect. One day we were at a race in Adelaide, and Dave Ryan walked past and said to give him a call at the factory. A few minutes later Ron came by and asked if Dave had spoken to me. So they asked me to come back and I was happy to do that.

above: **Chief truckie 'Tats' Cook is a man of many parts, including assigning many of the nicknames endured by his team-mates.**

right: **'Forks' Morrow handles the nozzle during refuelling, one of the most critical factors in effecting a speedy, and safe, pit stop.**

teamwork · **the race team**

159

The carefully parked trucks and their equipment-filled interiors effectively duplicate the pristinely efficient conditions at the factory.

'Ron once told me he wanted something done and I should make it idiot-proof. I always remember that. It was a classic statement. You check and double-check everything, leave nothing to chance. When you've won a lot of championships like us, you end up becoming even more professional. We double-check even more, because when you're into that system of winning, you pay that little bit more attention to everything, always trying to make it even better.

'You have to work harder here but in the end it pays off, because in making things better for the team you make them better for yourself. You get the most out of yourself. This attitude got me where I am today, what I've got today. I've got a brilliant marriage, a lovely daughter, nice house, all the luxuries of life. And it's all because I'm here doing a job and doing it right. Whatever it takes to get it done, you do it. And you do it happily because you know it works.'

Tats Cook, who was born in Canada and came to England when he was six, is a man of many parts. His tattoo-festooned limbs were inspired by his brother who was in the French Foreign Legion. Tats' body decorations were applied over a five-year period when he was a teenager. Now, he says, the novelty has worn off and he wishes the tattoos would too, but the laser treatment, which his brother has used to remove his, is a time-consuming and expensive business. These days Tats has other interests, one of which might qualify him to work with Lyndy Woodcock's catering department.

'I'm massively into cooking. I get more enjoyment out of spending half a day preparing it, then cooking it and serving it, than I do eating it. My family, and my mother and father, are my guinea pigs. My specialities are Chinese, Indian and Italian.'

That said, Tats notes that his McLaren job 'gobbles up the time – travelling to the races, doing the Grand Prix weekend, driving back to the factory, you're on the go all year round. As soon as we get back to the factory we take everything out of the trucks, clean it, polish it, service it, get it repaired, whatever needs to be done. Then we gather it all together, pack everything and hit the road again. In the winter months you stop travelling but you're always trying to improve on the year before, with better equipment, better garage design and so on. It's non-stop.'

The truckies are seldom seen in repose, but if a championship for perpetual motion was held Phil 'Shadwell' Williams would be a main contender. On the road Shadwell shares the driving with Tats. At the track he is in charge of the hand baggage and acts as the spares co-ordinator, looking after the hundreds of spare parts that are listed according to the gospel in Chris Robson's Bible. Shadwell also makes sure the pit stop area in front of the garage is shipshape, checking the set-up of the gantries, the positioning of the air guns, and the servicing and oiling of equipment.

Additionally, Shadwell is responsible for garage presentation and scurries around all weekend cleaning and polishing, keeping everything neat and tidy. In a pit stop he takes off the right front wheel and also changes the nose cone, should it be necessary. But during the race, until his services are required in a pit stop, Shadwell, the human dynamo, lies fast asleep on the garage floor in his helmet and full pit stop regalia. When his team-mates wake him up, with three laps to go before a car is due to come in for servicing, Shadwell switches into full action mode again.

'I know it sounds weird to nod off like that. But you're on the go from five in the morning – hard on it – then suddenly you're doing nothing. Bang. I'm finished. I've got two speeds. Flat out or nothing. I need a goal. I'll give 200 per cent for the goal and then I'll flake out.'

The original Shadwell was a character in a Welsh soap opera on television, and the version as played by Phil Williams on the Race Team is quirky and entertaining. A short, quick-witted busybody of a Welshman, he speaks that language and can also do a fair imitation of an air gun: 'Bbbrrrrrrrp!' His first job with McLaren was on the Test Team, but that lasted only five weeks because Shadwell needed the 'buzz' of racing. In addition to the many roles he plays at the races, Shadwell has appointed himself the team morale-booster.

'Shadwell' Williams – joker, champion morale booster and air gun imitator – is a study in perpetual motion.

'Joking and wisecracking. You have to keep the spirits up. You have to have wide shoulders, because it gets stressful. People can get pissed off when things go wrong with the car. After a while on the road people can get homesick. They might get a little snappy, but they'll apologize later. You can't take it to heart or you'll never last. Everybody gets on a bit of a downer from time to time. So you joke around a bit to get them up and running.'

One of Shadwell's closest mates among the truckies is Andrew 'Drew' Miller, who works on the tyres with Forks and Tats and mans the fire extinguisher during pit stops. As the seventh truckie, Drew is the designated 'floater', alternately relieving others from driving duties so they can enjoy the luxury of flying to a race. From a small village in Scotland, Drew followed his father into the army and served in a parachute regiment for more than 10 years. Drew has found that his military background was good training for serving with the McLaren troops.

'In the army, my regiment was very image-conscious, very proud. We set ourselves very high standards in presentation, equipment and discipline. So it just naturally translates to what we do here at McLaren. The standards are very high and everything is taken to its limit, whether it's with the car, the systems, anything we make. It's all well thought out and nicely put together. I was with another team for a while and one of the major reasons for coming here was that McLaren does it better. Take the pit equipment. Every single piece is designed to fit into the truck in a certain way. It's nicer to work with, to make it look good and be more professional. To a certain extent this scares people off. It doesn't seem a very friendly place to outsiders. But on the inside it's not that way at all. We have our fun.'

Derek 'Del' Jeanes, the oldest truckie, started working in racing in the early seventies and has been with McLaren since 1985. Besides driving a truck and providing general 'garage assistance' – charging batteries, looking after the lubrication stock and so on – he looks after the fuel for David Coulthard's car. Derek's longevity in the sport is based on a keen enthusiasm that runs in his family. His cousin Carl was known as 'The Streaker', because at a race at Thruxton, 'he ran naked in front of the crowd to win a bet for 50 quid so he could go Formula Ford racing. I used to help him' (fully clad, Del hastens to add) 'and that's how I got started in racing. And I still get a buzz from it. I like the whole atmosphere of it and the excitement that builds up over the weekend.'

Derek Jeanes first went racing before his fellow truckie, Kris de Groot, was born. When Derek joined McLaren, Kris was thinking about becoming a fireman (as his brother had been) when he grew up. Kris, known to his mates as 'Bruv', was introduced to motor racing by his father, who used to sell consumables to race teams at the circuits around England. As a teenager, Kris helped friends prepare a small saloon for club racing and after studying engine building at college he decided against it as a career and went racing instead. He joined McLaren in 1995 and now performs a variety of tasks, including taking off the left rear wheel during pit stops. In one of his other jobs, Kris continues the de Groot family tradition of dispensing consumables – paint, tape, tyre wraps, foam, bin liners and so on. He is also the senior fuel man looking after the refuelling trolleys, along with Del Jeanes, and is particularly responsible for looking after the fuel for Mika's car. As Kris explains, being attached to one car creates the kind of rivalry that produced Brian, The Snail.

'Drew' Miller finds his military background was good training for serving with the McLaren troops.

'It was a little plastic snail that you filled up with water and used like a water pistol. It fell out of a box of breakfast cereal one morning and somebody decided it would be a lucky omen. We called it Brian because it was an odd name for a snail. After qualifying, Brian would get filled up and each guy working on the slower car got sprayed with water. This went on for most of a season until one time after Mika's car was quickest in qualifying and we soaked the guys working on DC's car, then Mika went out of the race on the first lap. So we decided Brian's luck had run out and we would have to do away with him. We had a ceremony in the back of a truck. We burned him. A very undignified end for Brian.'

the race team · teamwork

the mechanics

'They're very good,' Mike Negline says of the truckies. 'They're hard workers and they know what they're doing. They have the garage well sorted by the time the boys come on Thursday, so we can get right to work.' The 'boys' are the mechanics and Mike is their chief – a man who seems to personify the team's highly developed work ethic.

His industriousness and the attention to detail for which he is noted (and for which he is sometimes called 'Niggling' Negline) were drummed into Mike at an early age. At home in Melbourne, Australia, their father instilled in Mike, his five brothers and his sister the belief that the way to make the most of their lives was to aspire to be the best at whatever they did and not accept anything less. Mike's pursuit of perfection began with a four-year apprenticeship as a mechanic, working at a garage that specialized in sportscars. Four years later Mike owned the company and soon also had on his cv an Australian sportscar championship, won in a Porsche that he had prepared.

The idea of combining his competitive instincts with his mechanical expertise seemed to Mike like a good way to get on in the world. His involvement in racing became full time in 1985 when he sold the garage business and moved to England. For several years he lived a nomadic existence, being involved in sportscar racing ventures in Japan, America and Europe. Then, in 1990, he applied for a job with McLaren and was hired within a week, starting as a Number Two mechanic on the Test Team.

'It was a bit intimidating,' Mike remembers of the time when he first came to McLaren. 'I'd never worked in a company with so many people and in such a big factory. To learn the way of working, the procedures of the company, was sort of worrying.'

Any worries Mike had about being able to fit in were quickly allayed – not least because of his penchant for saying 'No worries' in response to every request to get a

Chief mechanic Mike 'Hold the phone, Ruby' Negline (with team manager, Dave Ryan – *left***) personifies the team's highly developed work ethic.**

job done, no matter how difficult that job might be or how little time there is to do it. He quickly became a valued member of the team and soon found out how McLaren looks after its own. In 1991 he developed a serious thyroid condition that required an immediate operation. Though he had not yet even met Ron Dennis, the team leader arranged for Mike to be put up in a private hospital in London, where the operation was a success.

'It was all paid for by the team. I was really impressed that they actually thought that much of me to do it, even though I'd just started. And I thought if Ron and the management were prepared to go that far for me then I'd like to return the favour for them. It makes it easier to put everything you've got into it. And I do feel I give everything I've got. To me, that is part of the job. If you don't want to take responsibility and do the job, then don't do it.'

Mike's keen sense of responsibility led to rapid promotions and in 1995 he was appointed chief mechanic. At first, he recalls, there were some complaints about his style of leadership. 'Some of the boys said I was too militant, just telling them to do things instead of explaining why something had to be done then asking them to do it. There was a lot of pressure put on me to do maybe 10 jobs in an hour. The boys didn't know that side of it and I didn't take the time to explain it, so there was some resentment. I needed to learn how to manage people and with more experience I got better at it. Then I took a management course, which also helped.'

Mike also stage manages the pit stops, handling the all-important lollipop that signals the driver precisely where to stop and exactly when to leave. On his pit stop helmet is the nickname 'Ruby'. This name was given to him because one of the phrases he uses when asked to undertake a second task at the same time as he is busy with the first is: 'Hold the phone, Ruby'. Mike's conversation is peppered with other such Australianisms as: 'That's as much use as an ashtray on a motorbike', or '... mudflaps on a tortoise'; then there's 'busy as a Beirut brickie', or 'busy as a one-armed taxi driver'. Mike Negline is always busy and so are those under his command. 'My attitude is that this is a profession and it's part of my job to make sure that

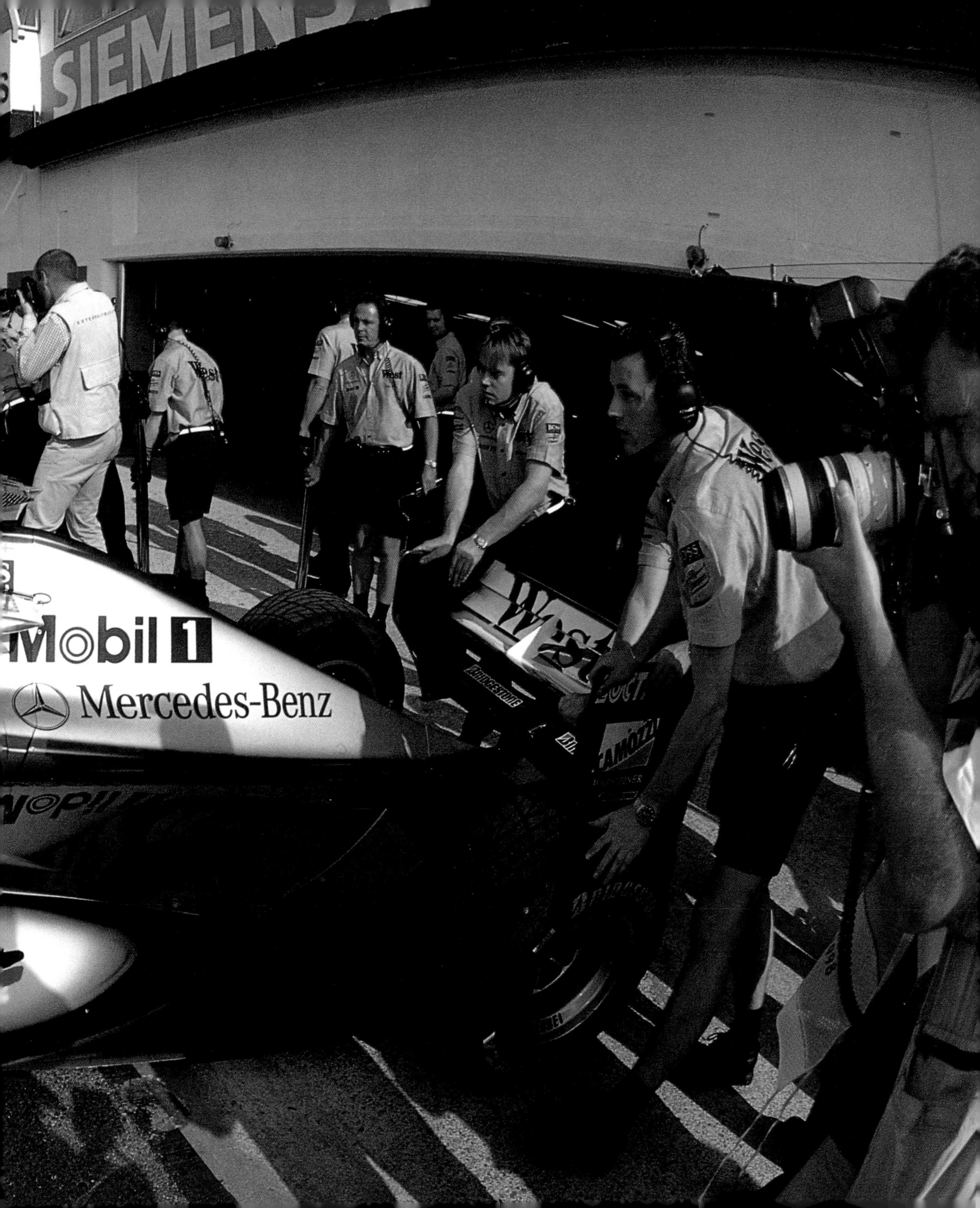
SIEMENS
Mobil 1
Mercedes-Benz
West

everything gets done professionally, to keep everybody busy and motivated. You can tell how the morale is, whether the boys are feeling up or down, by the way they're working and by the banter between them. If some of them get moody and aggravated you've got to be careful they don't take the others with them. Generally, there is quite a good spirit because we have some great characters here, like Wimp, Number One on DC's car. It says Gary Wheeler on his shirt but he's known as Wimp.'

Gary (who also handles the gun on the right front wheel in a pit stop) became 'Wimp' Wheeler when Forklift Morrow called his physical strength into question. 'Just after I came to McLaren, we were doing a test in Rio. Forks and I were working on Niki Lauda's car. I went to jack the thing up and just gave it a half-hearted effort because I

thought it had no fuel on board. But it had, and the car actually ended up in Forks' lap. Since then I've been Wimp.'

Wimp Wheeler, with McLaren since 1984, has always been a driver's mechanic, though he might have preferred reversing the roles, like his club-racing father. 'I think a lot of mechanics are frustrated racing car drivers, whether they admit it or not. But it would be hard to find a job that gives me as much satisfaction as this, though it's very demanding and you've got to have the right mental approach.

'Wimp' Wheeler (*left*)**, Number One mechanic on DC's car and a McLaren man since 1984 is, like his team-mates, a perfectionist.**

'You need to be organized, methodical in your head. You mustn't let trivial things upset you because you would just get shot to bits, otherwise. But most people who work at this job are perfectionists, anyway. And the reason you end up doing it, especially in a team like this, is because you like to do it the right way.'

Compared to the veteran Wimp Wheeler, the joint Number Two mechanics on DC's car are rookies – and they're both from Down Under. Like McLaren's founder, Stephen Giles comes from New Zealand, where he qualified as a mechanic and also did a bit of racing in karts and saloons before coming to England to work as a mechanic on touring cars. It wasn't that long ago that Stephen saw his first F1 car and he's only been with McLaren since 1996. Though he admits some of the mystery of the mechanical side of the sport has gone, the results of the race can have a profound effect.

'The highlight of my working career,' Stephen says, 'was when DC won in Melbourne in 1997. It was the first win for the team in some time and the feeling was fantastic. Then, in Canada, where we should have won that race but DC's car stalled, it was the lowest point. It really was like a kick in the guts. It hits you harder when it's your own car. There is a bit of a rivalry with the guys on Mika's car, but you feel happy for them when they get a good result and you feel badly if things go wrong after everybody has tried so hard.'

For Stephen (also called 'Al', because he looks like another Kiwi named Al who is no longer with the team) the highlight of the race weekend – 'the biggest adrenaline rush, probably the most enjoyable part of the job' – comes during the pit stops, when he operates the gun on the right rear wheel.

John Coleman of Ilmor, with 'Al' Giles and 'Patch' Vale. Patch loves the sound of the cars at the start. Al gets his biggest adrenaline rush in a pit stop.

Stephen's Australian workmate Peter Vale – alias 'Patch' (for the balding spot on the back of his head) – is also deeply involved in a pit stop, holding the refuelling hose. That chore, he admits, can send the adrenaline sky-rocketing, but for Patch Vale, a former refrigeration mechanic in Sydney: 'The high point of the Grand Prix weekend is the start of the race on Sunday afternoon. I lift my headphones up and just listen to all those cars take off. That's what it's all about! That's why you're there. Of course, it's also a great feeling when you've won a race, when you know all the effort you've put in has been rewarded.'

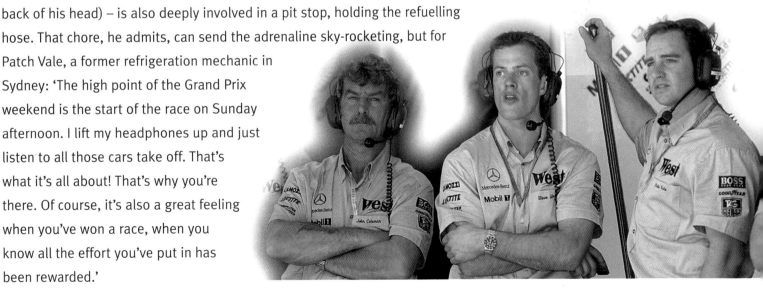

The mechanics on Mika's car are led by the Number One, Simon Moule, who came to McLaren in 1996 after his previous team ran out of money and folded. 'It was so new coming here,' Simon remembers, 'just a completely different world. I kept my head down and my mouth shut and got on with the job. Some people who have been here a long time and not worked for other teams take all this for granted. They don't know how good it is and what it's like down at the low end of the pit lane, worrying about what's happening from one race to the next and wondering if you'll still have a job. Here, you have nothing to worry about. You have to work a lot harder, but the money is good and you've got a job for life if you want it.'

But, as 'Simoni' notes (his mates say Simon looks like an Italian saloon car driver named Simoni), working on a front-running team with a chance of winning leads to

extra pressure to fulfil the expectations. 'The pressure builds up over the weekend so that by Sunday we all have our race face on. Although you prepare the car the same way every time, you get a bit uptight just before the start. You check, double-check and check, check, check everything. You can be a bit short with people – if they get on your back there is sometimes a "Shut up and get on with it" sort of thing.'

For a few seconds on race day, Simon becomes a pit crew man, handling the gun on the left front wheel. However, his main job is

Paul Cann, Stephen Giles and Simon Moule. The pressure on them builds up until Sunday, when they put their race faces on.

to oversee the preparation of Mika's car. 'The Number One is responsible for preparing the car the way the engineer wants it, making sure everything is done on time so the car is ready to go. A lot of what I do is overseeing the paperwork, just filling in numbers, which people joke about. "You don't need any spanners, just a pen or a highlighter." There's actually a bit more to it than that. As long as you've got two good Number Twos, you can rely on them.'

One of Simoni's Number Twos is Keith 'Wingnut' Barnard, who was just 20 years old when he started with McLaren in 1988. Keith's prominent ears prompted the nickname Wingnut, though he and Kris de Groot call each other 'Bruv'.

Wingnut began in the carpentry shop in the factory, moved on to fabrication, spent a year in the Test Team and joined the Race Team in 1993. During pit stops, he puts on the right rear wheel . 'We have our ups and downs,' he says of a mechanics job. 'The ups are winning, obviously. The downs, the worst part, are working very, very hard all weekend – late nights, two or three o'clock in the morning for three days – and then seeing both your cars not finish the race. After you've had a really hard weekend that can be very painful. You get depressed, though it wears off quite quickly and we all often joke about it. But it's no fun at the time.'

Joint Number Two mechanic on Mika's car is Ian Coates, who also operates the front jack in pit stops. Like Simon Moule, Ian was a refugee from a team that 'went down the tubes' and there was a bit of a culture shock when he came to McLaren in 1995. 'There are a lot of people here who have never been anywhere else. They don't know what it's like at the bottom of the pit lane. They don't know what it's like to struggle financially. They've always had it good. When you move around between teams you pick up experience by working with all kinds of people, young people, old people, and you pick up tips and bits and pieces along the way. That way you can bring some new thinking into a team. But there is a definite McLaren way of doing things.'

One of the things McLaren does not allow is music in the garage. Up and down the pit lane, especially when the mechanics are working late at night, the loud music blaring from several garages makes it sound like simultaneous rock concerts are in progress. Rock music connoisseurs at McLaren say they don't mind not having their own music because it's plenty loud enough in the other garages. But the long-standing no-music-at-McLaren rule was imposed in the belief that the music would undermine the strict military-style discipline for which the team is famous. And that's fine with John 'Johnny O' Ostrowski, a Number Two mechanic on the spare car, the left rear wheel gun operator in pit stops, a McLaren man for over a dozen years, and before that a veteran of seven years in the army.

'Wingnut' Barnard's job has its ups and downs. The ups are when the team wins. The downs, after working night and day, are when a car fails to finish.

'I know people have the impression that we're the most regimented team,' Johnny O agrees. 'But I think it seems to work quite well. I've always worked at McLaren so perhaps I'm biased. But if you look up and down the pit lane there aren't many who've won as much as we have. Even through the hard times we managed to maintain the image and that discipline, to keep it a good environment to work in. Sure, people moan about it. I do. It's part of the job to moan!'

For Adrian Burgess, senior mechanic on the spare car, and the rear jack man in pit stops, joining McLaren in 1991 fulfilled a long-held dream. Known to the others as 'ATB', after his initials, he sometimes refers to himself as Adrian 'Top Bollocks' Burgess. As a boy he had a paper route and when racing magazines like *Autosport* were included in his deliveries ATB admits householders had to wait a while before they got them.

'I used to open up the magazines and have a look. I decided then, probably when I was about 10 years old, that I wanted to be in Formula 1 and I really wanted to be at McLaren. They were doing quite well at the time, very successful. So the goal was always to get here and it's great to be involved now.'

above: **'Turbo' Lunnon's family watch the races on television. When Turbo's team wins they celebrate with champagne, while he strips down yet another gearbox.**

The team that Adrian Burgess admired as a boy has changed considerably, as Mark Lunnon points out. Nicknamed 'Turbo' because of his fondness for turbo-charged road cars, and now the gearbox mechanic on Mika's car and the 'taker off' of the right rear wheel in pit stops, he has been with McLaren for a dozen years and on the Race Team for nine years.

right: **Mechanics Ian Coates and 'Johnny O' Ostrowski, respectively, also operate the front jack and the left rear wheel gun in pit stops.**

'When I joined McLaren, we were only 84 people,' Turbo recalls. 'Now there are hundreds – more of them, it seems, every week. In a way, you sort of lose that personal feel, but there is no question we operate as a team much better now. Things are much more structured, better organized, very defined departments. And the team spirit is still there.'

The McLaren spirit extends beyond the Race Team, away from the circuits and back into the homes of the families of the team personnel. On race day, Turbo Lunnon's wife and his parents sit transfixed in front of their television sets, waiting for a glimpse of their hero taking the right rear wheel off in pit stops. 'They watch every single race. They haven't missed one since I started at McLaren. And when I started working on Mika's car they actually kept a bottle of champagne waiting for him to win. It gathered a bit of dust until he won that last race of '97. Then there was a big celebration.'

Trevor Lawes is the gearbox mechanic on DC's car. 'Trevooor' (from the way he speaks) has been a gearbox man as long as Turbo Lunnon, during which time the particular items of their mechanical concern have hardly ever failed. Trevor, who also puts the left front wheel on in pit stops, can only remember a handful of occasions when gearbox problems caused a car's retirement from a race.

Gavin Beresford handles DC's pit board, while Gerry Good (*background*) keeps Mika informed of his progress on the track.

'But it can be quite tense when you're waiting in the garage. If you hear a message on the radio that DC's having a problem with a downshift or something like that, you think: "Oh, no!" But most of the time it's something else, maybe engine-related, so you give a sigh of relief. It's better for us, but then you start feeling badly for the other guys.'

If something should go wrong on David Coulthard's car one of the first to hear about it is Gavin Beresford, who handles DC's pit board on the pit wall. Every lap the car is on the track, during practice and qualifying as well as in the race, Gavin flashes DC the latest information.

'There is a lot of scrambling around between laps. I work in conjunction with Pat Fry (David's race engineer) and Dave Ryan, who actually gives me the times to put on the board. Normally the board shows your car's position, the lap it's on, and how far behind and ahead of the cars closest to it. It gets pretty frantic when you're at a track that has a short lap and you've only got a few seconds to get the numbers on the board.'

Gavin doesn't mind when things get hectic; in fact, he thrives on those emergencies that bring his talents as the team's fabricator into play. Before he assumed that role he spent six years in the research and development department in the factory, where he enjoyed the experimental aspect of the work. His speciality now is effecting on-the-spot repairs, making temporary modifications and cobbling up solutions to unforeseen problems that might crop up at the circuit. Should an exhaust system be overheating a piece of carbon fibre bodywork, or should a component not have enough clearance or a driver have trouble with his seat fitting perfectly, Gavin springs into action.

'Gav' Beresford (*centre*) **also springs into action when emergencies call upon his talents as the team fabricator. He thrives on panic situations.**

'I must admit I prefer being hands-on in a panic situation. You have to react instinctively and solve the problem, then and there. Often, there is a very limited timespan before the car has to run again, and you know it has to get back out there, regardless. It's a nice sense of achievement when you just manage to get it done and the car goes out of the garage on time. And when it goes out again, the old heart's going and you're shaking a bit and trying to get your breath back, that does give me a buzz. I've done my job. That's what I'm here for.'

Gavin comes from a long line of motor racing Beresfords. His father became involved in the mechanical side of the sport over 50 years ago and joined Bruce McLaren's F1 team soon after it was founded. He stayed there for many years and now runs the composite department of the Penske IndyCar team.

'My father always said to me, and also to my two brothers who are now in motor racing, "Be very careful when you get into it, because it's very demanding time-wise and it can be quite stressful, hard on the family and everything else. But it can be very rewarding." '

Gavin and his wife have three young Beresfords, two boys and a girl, and when the man of the house is away at the races he sometimes gets homesick. 'But the one good thing is the children know their grandfather and their uncles are in motor racing. They've grown up with it and understand. And if they ever wanted to get into motor racing I would leave it entirely up to them. I wouldn't advise them against it because it's provided us with a very good standard of living. And if they asked my advice for a team to be with I would not hesitate to say McLaren. Because of the working standards and everything else I think it is head and shoulders above any other team.'

Gavin is sometimes known as 'Waspy' Beresford to his team-mates. 'It's not something I am proud of but I guess I occasionally let my emotions get the better of me and I can sting, verbally at least. If I'm thinking hard about how to solve a problem and someone is buggering around, or whatever, I can be caught off guard and lash out. Then somebody like Shadwell, whom I like immensely, will come around and there will be a light-hearted moment. We're a very hard-working bunch and if everyone was absolutely strait-laced and too serious it would be a boring place to work. You need these characters to really uplift things once in a while.'

the engineers

One of the strongest McLaren characters is one of the team's longest serving members: Tyler Alexander. The further up you go in the hierarchy of the team, the fewer the nicknames, but if Tyler (who is sometimes identified by his initials 'TJA') had one it might be 'Groucho', as in Groucho Marx, the celebrated American comedian noted for his acerbic wit. Besides the vast experience that makes him among the most valued members of McLaren's engineering staff – he is currently embedded-systems engineer on Mika's car – Tyler is the team's resident loveable curmudgeon. This is an unofficial post earned through his propensity for delivering pithy, often profane, observations that lighten up the serious business of

Engineers Steve Hallam (*left*) and Tyler Alexander. Tyler, a founding director of McLaren in 1963, lightens up the serious business of racing with pithy comments.

F1 racing, which according to Tyler's definition is: 'Just sorting through the horseshit looking for the horse.'

Tyler (whose ruggedly handsome countenance has been compared by admiring females to a Hollywood-style American cowboy) first rode into the F1 fray in 1963, when he became a founding director and one of the original shareholders of Bruce McLaren Motor Racing Limited. In his native America, he studied aeronautical engineering – and he might have gone into that field, or another, but he chose F1 racing, a sport he has described as being 'like an over-bred cocker spaniel'.

'I could be the lavatory attendant at London Zoo. Some people are interested in ice-cream cones. I'm interested in racing cars. You're either in this business, or you're not. There are good days and there are bad days. If you went into a corner and cried every time there was a bad day, you might as well stay at home. If you're not winning, faith healing won't cure it, you just have to keep working harder. Winning is like the frosting on the cake. The object of the exercise is to build the car, race it, go home, fix it, then go racing again. Racing is just a plain old bunch of very difficult, complicated, hard work that's a pain in the ass.'

Yet Tyler (who says 'racing takes up too much time, too much of the time') has managed to tolerate the pain in his posterior for more than a third of a century. 'One of the major reasons is that every two weeks you find out whether you've done a good job or not. I'd probably do this for nothing. The money is just to put up with all the bullshit.'

'I think as much as the guys may not like admitting it, they love this job and that's why they keep coming back.' This is Anton Stipinovich, embedded-systems engineer on David Coulthard's car. A South African who was involved in various forms of racing for 13 years before joining McLaren in 1997, Anton talks about how a passion for the sport can take over a life.

'You don't have a normal life, because you're away from home for four to 10 days at a time. And when you go home you have trouble adjusting to it. A lot of racing people have no home life, or a difficult one. But no one is forcing us to be here, so we're doing it because we want to. Maybe we're stupid, but I think everyone enjoys it. At the end of a season you get different views. People will say this is their last year and they're never going back again. And then after a bit of a holiday they begin to get anxious to go racing again.'

Anton thinks 'the English have a very special sense of humour, and I'm not English. Sometimes it's funny and sometimes all the gobbiness, taking the piss, is hard to take. I prefer to concentrate on what I'm doing and then being gobby when the work is over. But 95 per cent of these guys are fantastic. There is so much experience. It's an awesome team.'

Another crew member is Paul 'Bass' Cann, a former British Aerospace employee who, 10 years ago, turned his talents to working on the McLaren cars that fly

teamwork · **the race team**

on the ground. Among his other responsibilities, Paul is on standby during pit stops to perform the duties of 'rat box' cleaner (removing any debris from the air intakes) and/or clean up any fuel spills.

Paul's main job is as data analysis technician on Mika's car and much of his view of a race weekend is seen through a monitor where the constant stream of telemetry data, relayed to the pits by the 100 sensors on the car, provides intimate insights into what a driver is doing – through the throttle position, gear changes, steering wheel position and the amount of brake pressure applied, as well as the road speed of the car. The data is collected in three ways: in real time, as the car travels around the circuit; in bursts, as each car passes the pits; and via hard-wire links, when the car returns to the garage and the data is downloaded into the computers.

'They can't hide anything,' Paul says of Mika and David. 'Everything is there – a missed shift or braking point, a lift off – and whatever they do is always logged and recorded. When we do an overlay on the screen, comparing the two drivers, the main thing is to see where they're gaining or losing time. If they say they have understeer or oversteer in a corner, then the engineers can adjust the set-up accordingly. It's especially exciting for us in qualifying when you can see something that might help them go quicker.'

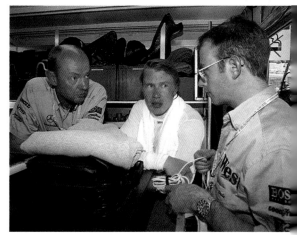

Mark Slade, formerly a data analysis engineer on Mika's car, was promoted in 1998 to become his race engineer. When Mark was studying Mechanical Engineering in Aberdeen he was a fan of the flamboyant Ferrari driver, the late Gilles Villeneuve. When Mark examines the data from the car of McLaren's Flying Finn he can spot familiar traits.

Senior race engineer Steve Hallam (*left***), Mika and Mark Slade, Mika's race engineer. Data shows that the Flying Finn is on the limit a lot of the time.**

'In Mika's data you can see he almost abuses the car sometimes to get it around a corner – the way Villeneuve used to do. His driving style is quite sort of on the limit. Mika has immense natural talent and the flair that Villeneuve showed. And when he picks up the bull by the horns, the way he can do, I don't think there is anybody that's going to stop him.'

On the telemetry the engineers
can monitor everything that
happens in the cockpit. Racers
to the core, they appreciate
hard-trying drivers.

In 1991 Mark started at McLaren as an engineer working in Neil Oatley's Design Department on engine ancillaries and hydraulic systems. But it was always his ambition to go racing and in 1994 he joined the Race Team.

'After working on Mika's car through '96 and '97 I learned Mika's ways, and came to respect his opinion and enjoy working with him. A lot of what we have to say concerns technicalities, but you have to choose your words carefully so that the driver understands and you don't introduce any unnecessary worries into what you're talking about. And sometimes they need a bit of guidance. I think psychology does play quite a large part in the whole exercise between the driver and the race engineer.'

Pat Fry, DC's race engineer, agrees that the job includes 'being a psychologist, trying to work out when to say the right thing to the driver, when to calm him down, when to leave him alone, when to help him. David is fairly sensible, level-headed, calm, cool and collected, which is also the way I've got to be doing the job I do. You might be the most fucked-up person in the whole garage, but you can't show it because it's contagious and you don't want it to spread. You've got to try and hold it all together.'

Like many of his co-workers, Pat, who joined McLaren in 1992 after several years with the Benetton team, is a racing enthusiast who made the sport his profession. While studying as an electronics engineer he built motorbikes as a hobby, then put his handiwork to the test by thrashing the bikes around at speed.

Pat worked in electronics for the Ministry of Defence, which was interesting but only for about one-tenth of his time. 'The rest was boring paperwork. I'm not really a pencil man. This is one job where you get straight into it and don't stop. There's nowhere else where you have a race weekend by the end of which you know whether you did okay or not. And it's not just based on whether we won or lost. You can judge yourself, as well. I'm my hardest critic and you have to ask yourself: "Did I get the best out of what we had today?" The ideal is to walk away thinking, "Yes, I've done the best I can."

DC's race engineer Pat Fry constantly tries to get the most from himself, as well as his driver. Psychology often comes into play.

'If you're doing the best you can at all these events – 16 or 17 races a year, 20 to 25 tests, and the engineers go to both – it's a hell of a lot of time and it takes a lot out of you. I'm not saying I don't enjoy it, because I do. Otherwise I wouldn't do it. I've found something I can be good at and that I quite enjoy. It can be fun.'

An example of the lighter side of the serious business of race engineering is provided by Steve Hallam, who was promoted to the position of senior race engineer in 1998 after several seasons engineering Mika Hakkinen's car. Steve, a supremely well-organized person, prepares the extensive job lists that determine the duty-packed agenda for the engineers on race weekends. As a joke, to end the list of first-day tasks that leave the personnel with scarcely an idle minute from dawn to dusk, one year at Monaco Steve wrote a final instruction for the mechanics: 'Buy engineers gin and tonic in the bar, and sit with feet up watching the sun go down over the sea.'

From finishing the list with 'something silly', Steve went on to replace it with a historical quiz, coming up with three or four questions concerning whatever race the team was at. If the job lists were issued at the factory before the team left for the event, the fierce competition to come up with answers to Steve's quiz had people poring over history books.

Over the years Steve Hallam has been a part of an impressive amount of F1 history. His interest in racing was first piqued in 1963, when the great Scottish driver Jim Clark was flourishing with Team Lotus. Led by the heroic exploits of the driver, Steve's attention drifted to a fascination with the technicalities of the sport, the designing and the running of cars. By 1968 Steve had decided the racing life was for him and he began methodically to structure his career in that direction. In 1975, armed with a degree in Automobile Engineering, he applied to many different F1 teams but found there were no vacancies for inexperienced engineers. He went to work for Aston Martin in development engineering, but never lost sight of his original ambition. Finally, in 1981, a response to an advertisement in an engineering publication brought him to Team Lotus and the career of Steve Hallam, race engineer, began.

Working with the late Colin Chapman, Lotus founder and engineering genius, Steve began by running Nigel Mansell's car. After Chapman died, in 1982, the team was less successful but for three years at Lotus Steve had the invaluable experience of working with Ayrton Senna, then in the formative stages of his brilliant career. When Senna moved to McLaren he told his trusted race engineer he would welcome the opportunity to work with him again. That opportunity came in 1991 when Neil Oatley persuaded Steve to come to McLaren. There, Steve found himself at the opposite end of the spectrum.

'You were joining a World Championship-winning team that was unbelievably well-funded compared to Lotus. Whereas at Lotus in the latter years you were happy if you got a few points, at McLaren you were distressed if you weren't winning. There seemed to be a huge amount of confidence in what you were doing. The issue of finishing second – of not winning – simply wasn't there. It was inspiring because it

Steve Hallam knows, and has played a part in, a lot of F1 history. As a youth Jim Clark was his favourite. Steve later engineered cars for the great Ayrton Senna.

made you push all the harder in what you were doing. You couldn't allow your personal performance to slip behind the others. You wanted to step up to their level and it was fabulous!'

His previous experience of not winning makes Steve better prepared than some of his colleagues for the inevitable losing that every F1 team must endure. It isn't any easier for him to take, but Steve notes that, for engineers especially, it is important to set an example to keep up the morale, similar to the way a race engineer must speak to his driver during a race.

For the hard-working engineers, idly sipping a gin and tonic and watching the sun go down is mostly a daydream.

'You want to communicate in a clear, confident way. You don't want any shadow of doubt in your voice. The issue is maintaining one's cool and discipline, and keep doing your job right, especially when you're behind. We say to the mechanics: "You keep doing what you're doing now and it will happen." We say the same thing to the drivers. I suppose it's like the coach of a football team being down two goals at half time. All you can do is tell them to keep playing their best and it will happen.'

When it does happen, when McLaren wins, the engineers led by Steve Hallam often seem not to be especially moved. Steve suggests the collective solemnity may be related to the stressful circumstances race engineers must endure and the fatigue that follows. For the engineers, idly sipping a gin and tonic and watching the sun go down is mostly a daydream. What they really want to do at the end of a Grand Prix day is sleep.

'At the end of the day you carry the can; you are responsible for much of what happens. You are in charge of the cars at the circuit. You work with the driver and the crew of people within the team to get the best performance over the weekend. There is tension and pressure as the hours and minutes tick by before you become

Some of the personnel on the 1997 Race Team...

left: **On Mika's car (from the left): Mark Lunnon, Keith Barnard, Kris de Groot, Ian Webb (Ilmor), Mark Slade, Phil Collins (Ilmor), Steve Hallam, Paul Cann, Roger Higgins (Ilmor), Steve Cook, Gerry Good, Nick Lee (Ilmor), Ricky Taylor and Simon Moule.**

centre: **On the T-car (from the left): Tony Harlow (Mobil), Adrian Burgess, Ian Coates, Alastair Hawkeswood (Ilmor), John Coleman (Ilmor), Yukihiro Nagumo (Kenwood), Takaesi Yosiaka (Kenwood), Eric Johnson (Mobil), Jo Ramirez, Anton Stipinovich, Paul Simpson, Jonathon Ostrowski, Gavin Beresford, Drew Miller and Phil Williams.**

right: **On DC's car (from the left): Stephen Giles, Paul Monaghan, Steve Morrow, Mark Grey (Ilmor), Dave Ryan, Trevor Lawes, Pete Vale, Dieter Gundel, Tim White (Ilmor), Derek Jeanes, Gary Wheeler and Mike Negline.**

operational. You've attempted to be as thorough as possible before you start running and then there comes a point when everything just goes calm. It's physically tough; a lot of endurance is required and there is fatigue when it's over.'

Team Manager Dave Ryan has been experiencing the rigours of McLaren race weekends since 1974, when he was a teenager fresh off the boat from New Zealand. Dave is known within the team as 'Von Ryan' – from *Von Ryan's Express*, the film about a train in World War Two – and he signs documents that way. Keeping the McLaren train on track at the race so that it delivers the goods requires him to cover everything from the locomotive to the guard's van. For his job of organizing the efforts of the engineers, the mechanics and the truckies, Dave has evolved his own management style.

Team manager Dave 'Von' Ryan (with DC), a McLaren man since 1974, gets his motivation from the team effort that produces victory.

'The way I approach it is to keep very much in the background. I don't force myself to the front. We've got a lot of very good people working here. A lot of them have been around a long time, and between us we can cover just about every eventuality. So, mostly it's just a question of watching what happens, putting things right when they are not happening as they should be. Generally, it's a matter of keeping on top of things without standing in front of the garage waving my arms and shouting "do this, that and the other". I think you've got to respect people for what they're doing.

'Everybody here puts in a huge amount of effort. Sometimes it's hard for the truckies and the mechanics because they don't really know what's going on and often there's not enough time to explain it to them. At times they get pretty pissed off about various things, and you can understand why. Sometimes we drive them very hard. And from the engineers' point of view, they've got a long hard struggle all the time, looking for the competitiveness and keeping it. People can get down, depressed. When they do you just try to turn it around, and you do it by whatever means possible – whether it's saying the right thing, or explaining the problem, putting it right, making it easier for them.

'It's hard to make it all come together, so that when it does, it's a tremendous feeling. And that's where the motivation comes from. It's very, very satisfying when the cars run well, when you see your drivers doing a good job, when you see the crew doing good pit stops. There's a sharing of enthusiasm. And when you win, everybody is delighted. It's fantastic. It's a team effort.'

During the race Dave Ryan works on the pit wall with Pat Fry, running David Coulthard's car. When they call DC in for a pit stop the man who cleans the visor on his helmet is, by his own admission, the highest paid windscreen wiper in the world! 'I don't need to do it, but I still like to be involved, to get my hands out there. I guess I'm just a racer at heart.' This is Jo Ramirez, who is paid to be the team co-ordinator. In some ways he is also the team's heart and soul.

'Señor Jo' or 'Papa Jo' as he is called, left his native Mexico in 1962 and has been racing around the world ever since. His official duties at McLaren, where he has been since 1983, include handling all the logistics of travel and transportation for the team and its equipment, liaising with race organizers (he speaks five languages), working with TMMS as an intermediary with sponsors and so on. Beyond that Jo thinks part of his job 'is making sure that the team is up and motivating people all the time. I'm a very easy character, most always happy. Having said that, whenever we get down, or we lose a race or something, maybe I suffer more than the rest. I may just want to go in the corner and cry, or pack my things and go away. But 10 minutes later I sort of look ahead – be optimistic about the future, and try to make the rest of the people feel the same.

'I think it is always important to look forward in this business. With motor racing, when you win there is a fantastic feeling, but the lows are much lower than a normal business. You have to be strong and fight for it. And it is contagious. When Ayrton Senna was driving for us he magnetized the whole team to follow him. He was very strong with the team, very strong with himself. If we did something wrong he would really let us know. If he did something wrong, he would punish himself. He felt very deeply about the team.

'You know, people here don't always show it, but they feel very personally about the team. There is a lot of loyalty here. You see the faces at McLaren don't change very often, but sometimes you hear talk from the outside that the team is cold. They say that about Ron. He seldom smiles because he's just very focused on everything he does. But deep inside, he is a man with a big heart. He is a man with a lot of feelings, and definitely feelings for the people that work with him. If you are loyal to him, he will always be loyal to you.

Mika is noted for being a man of few words and usually lets his heavy right foot do the talking. But when he hears anyone criticizing the team, the Flying Finn is quick to respond and becomes quite voluble.

'Anybody who thinks McLaren is cold should just talk to any of our drivers. Unfortunately, they will not be able to speak to Ayrton, but they could talk to Alain Prost. Alain felt that McLaren was like a family team, where the driver is considered very much part of the family. We always try to make them happy. I think it is an important part of my job to have the drivers content, to consider their feelings, to give them everything they need. If they have no worries, they can just get in the car and do their job.'

the drivers

Mika Hakkinen was born in Helsinki, Finland, in 1968, a few months after Bruce McLaren won the first F1 race in a McLaren car. While Mika was busy winning the Finnish karting championship – five times through to 1986 – McLaren was establishing itself as a major force in F1. Mika went on to become a champion in Formula Ford and in British Formula 3, before joining Team Lotus in 1991. His arrival at McLaren in 1993 coincided with the team establishing what was then the record for the most wins by any team in F1 history.

'When I first came here I don't mind telling you it was frightening. I was going to a team which was absolutely the dream for many drivers. A fantastic team. Extremely fantastic history. Ayrton was there at the time, so it was just extremely exciting. There was a lot to learn, so it was good that I started as test driver, and that gave me time to learn.

'It was like going to school, learning how the team worked. You have to be on the absolute edge of everything here all the time, and you learn fast. It is exciting because it develops you enormously as a person. I think what you learn most is to work closer with other people, understand the way they work and how they think. That is an important lesson. The better you work together, the stronger you are.'

Mika is noted for being a man of few words and usually lets his heavy right foot do the talking. But when he is asked about life at McLaren, or when he hears anyone criticizing the team, the Flying Finn is quick to respond and becomes quite voluble.

Mika relies on the team's sense of humour – "some of it a bit strange" – to relieve the stress from the very serious business of racing.

'It is completely rubbish to think McLaren is cold and does not have character! I think they have much more character than any team in the paddock. This team has people who have been working here for years. And they're still motivated, dedicated, and they have great character, a good sense of humour, and they know the business like nobody else. It is the most professional team. They work hard, like crazy, and it is such a pleasure to work in this environment. It is very, very special, and this is because of the people in it.

'This is an extremely tough business, a very serious business. Very stressful. So you have to be able to have fun and relax, otherwise you will burn yourself out. You have to laugh sometimes, even if you have problems. That's what the English guys say to me. They have a good sense of humour. There are a lot of Kiwis and Australians here, too. Their sense of humour is a bit strange.

"There are no superstars here.
All the truckies, the mechanics,
the engineers, the drivers –
everybody is equal."

Mika Hakkinen

"The team environment has
always been very important
to me... I need to feel part
of the team."

David Coulthard

'But when the boys are doing their job, they are seriously hard workers. And they know it is important for the driver to see they are serious when they are working on one of the fastest cars in the world. If they are not taking their responsibility seriously, they cannot get the confidence of the driver. I would not get in the car and go flat out around the corners if I didn't believe in the team. You have to trust each other to do the job. There are no superstars here. All the truckies, the mechanics, the engineers, the drivers – everybody is equal. When I stand on the podium I don't think I'm there because I'm the best. It's teamwork and everybody is working together in the organization.

Mika's several years of sacrifice and dedication were rewarded with his first F1 victory – at the 1997 European Grand Prix.

teamwork · **the race team**

'McLaren may look scary to outsiders because it is so well organized, but Ron cares a lot about his drivers. Even though McLaren is a big company, it is a very human connection that I have with Ron and the team.'

When talking about his close relationship with Ron and the team, Mika's usual Nordic reserve softens. He speaks from the heart, especially when he recalls the time he nearly gave his life for the McLaren cause. The accident, caused by a punctured tyre during practice for the 1995 Australian Grand Prix in Adelaide, left Mika with serious head injuries. During his rehabilitation, Mika credits the support of those closest to him as the main factor leading to a complete recovery.

'The most important thing was people. I got an enormous amount of letters from fans around the world, which really inspired me. But the biggest help was from the person

At the start of every race Mika and DC carry with them the hopes and dreams of the 300-plus people on the team.

closest to me: my girlfriend [now his wife], Erja. She was with me all the time, giving psychological support. My mental strength was improved because I could talk to this one person all the time. I was in great pain, and she understood my suffering and could do something about it, by just being there and talking to me. She was always there.

'My parents were with me when I was in hospital in Australia and they were also a big help. And then my manager Keke Rosberg [a former McLaren driver], Ron Dennis and Ron's wife Lisa – all these people made my life easier by organizing things for me. They didn't think just about today and tomorrow. They were planning ahead for a few months, so that everything went smoothly.'

Many in the team joined Mika in shedding tears when he won his first F1 race at the end of the 1997 season in Jerez, Spain. The victory was arranged, when David Coulthard was asked to let him by, mainly as a thank you for Mika's sacrifice and dedication to McLaren, and also to give him the confidence to win again.

When Mika won the next race, the 1998 Australian Grand Prix, he was again indebted to his team-mate, who honoured an agreement they had made before the start. According to their pact, made so as to not risk an accident or overstress the new cars whose reliability was not yet proven, whichever driver went into the first corner first should win the race. Second into the corner, DC later took the lead from Mika, then handed it back to him at the finish. Mika was moved by his team-mate's sacrifice. 'I must say what David did in Melbourne was absolutely fantastic and I will never forget that.'

Like Mika, his Scottish team-mate David Coulthard is a dedicated team player. Born in 1971, DC started racing 11 years later, winning his way through various formulae until an opportunity arose in F1 in 1994, by way of the tragic events that afflicted the sport that year. Then racing in F3000, DC was also test driving for Williams, who called him up to replace the late Ayrton Senna. In his second year at Williams, DC dedicated his first F1 victory, at the Portuguese Grand Prix, to his parents, who had supported him throughout his formative racing years.

'The team environment has always been very important to me,' DC says. 'I'm not one of those people who is able to just walk in, say a cold hello to everyone, get in the car and do the job. I need to feel part of the team. I grew up karting with a motorhome full of 10 people. In Formula Ford I was with a lot of people. When I was with Paul Stewart Racing in Formula 3 and Formula 3000, I lived near the factory and went there nearly every day. In a Formula 1 team there are many more people and the system doesn't allow you to get that close, at least right away.'

DC's home village of Twynholm in Scotland has approximately the same number of people as McLaren International employs. When he came to the team in 1996 he had a preconceived notion of what to expect.

David 'DC' Coulthard, the 38th McLaren driver since the team began, has been racing since he was 11 years old.

'From outside McLaren it looks so regimented and so clinical, almost to the point that it has no personality. On the inside, of course, it is different, because you get to know the personalities of the team. And they're all individuals with their own characters. Together, they make up the team, but there is something different about anyone who can lead in their field the way this team has. They seem a little bit eccentric in some way, but that must be part of the leading, rather than following.'

When DC won his first race for McLaren in Australia in 1997, ending the team's winless streak that had lasted 50 races, he wept. 'It meant a hell of a lot to the team. I never thought I would be so emotional as to cry in a racing car, but on the slowing down lap I did. It was a great feeling to be able to reward these guys who put their heart and soul into the team.

previous page: **DC is a popular winner. His victories are also celebrated in his home village in**

Scotland, where the population is about the size of McLaren International.

'Take Jo Ramirez, for instance. He wears his heart on his sleeve. He has a lot of passion for the sport. Even though he's been around a long time, and tells good stories from the past, sometimes he seems like a little boy who's just seen his first racing car – which is good, because he gives his enthusiasm to those around him in the team.

'Dave Ryan, I've never seen him get angry. He's very even tempered. When he's making a point he's able to do it in a very soft voice without slamming his fist down on the table, but you know exactly you're being told something. And I think that's a credit to him. I'm not that good at controlling my emotions. I admire the fact that he is able to do that.

'Mike Negline is another one of those guys you never really see upset. Nothing seems to be too much trouble for him. Now as a driver, the people you deal with regularly are going to be slightly more friendly than they might to others. You don't want to piss a driver off. But these guys are genuine.

'Ron has a very dominant personality and sometimes it's hard to get your opinion across when you have someone as forceful and powerful as that. But we have frank discussions and I've managed to hold my own. There is no question it's his team and you can't quarrel with his results.

'Norbert Haug is definitely the key to why Mercedes are so enthusiastic about their motorsport programme. Having met the various board members and seen the set-up in Stuttgart, you have to say that Norbert is largely responsible for the Mercedes involvement with the team and for keeping up the enthusiasm. He is a good person to have on side. Norbert's been honest with me when we've had some difficult times, and I've been honest with him. And I believe that is the key to maintaining any relationship – being able to be honest.

"I believe most F1 drivers would race for nothing if the prevailing economic situation removed the means of paying them. In these days of million dollar retainers, one fundamentally forgets these guys enjoy driving."
Ron Dennis

'As a driver you're naturally closest to your race engineer. Pat Fry and I get along well. I'm very happy with the relationship. Again, he's fairly laid back. He can get fiery

when something's upsetting him. He's not afraid to say something that may not sit comfortably with those who would prefer nothing be said.

'I've never come in to Pat and tried to tell him there was a problem with the car when I knew the problem was with me. And he's never been shy about saying it when he thinks the problem is with me. He does it in a diplomatic way, saying something like "Look, if you want to do better it's my opinion you're doing this wrong and you should try that." I trust Pat and I really believe he knows my strengths and my weaknesses.

'You can judge a lot about a team by its truckies. And we've got some really good ones. Take Forks Morrow. He's a great guy. He's our fuel man, and my tyre man as well. He is a main reason why we're good in pit stops. Any team can get the tyres changed in four and a half, five seconds, but the key to the stop is how quick the fuel man gets the nozzle on. Forks is tall, he's got the leverage and he's got the weight. He's got Patch Vale behind him on the hose, another big guy. The whole crew works together like clockwork. My win at Monza in '97 was a direct result of a superior stop. I don't think they get enough credit for it, but when you have these guys behind you on a race weekend you've already got a head start.'

grand

prix weekend

"Motor racing is an absolutely essential motivational force in my life. I love it. I love the adrenaline. I love the challenge. I love the competition."

RON DENNIS

the timetable

On a Grand Prix weekend the Race Team's activities are centred around a strict schedule set to meet the deadlines imposed by the timetable that determines when the cars go out on the track. These occasions, on Friday, Saturday and Sunday, become progressively more critical and the pressure on the team mounts accordingly. Including practice, qualifying, the warm-up and the race itself the track is open to the cars for up to six hours, but in reality the whole weekend amounts to a race against time.

The battle with the ticking clock begins with two hours of practice on Friday, an anxious time when the first indications of the state of competitiveness become apparent. Tension mounts during the 90 minutes of

The weekend starts quickly, then speeds up. The cars will be timed to the thousandth of a second. The garage will be spotless throughout.

practice on Saturday morning, when final preparations are made for the critical hour that follows. At one o'clock in the afternoon the qualifying session begins. In this pressure-packed 60 minutes the times set by the cars are clocked to the thousandth of a second to determine the all-important grid positions for the race. The team then has 24 hours to prepare for the main event.

On Sunday morning the 30-minute warm-up session serves as a dress rehearsal for that most critical time of all: the up to two hours of nerve-wracking, wheel-to-wheel racing that puts the team to the ultimate test.

Throughout the weekend the Race Team works according to an operational structure that has largely been determined beforehand. Built into this systematic approach is an elasticity to accommodate the uncertainties and changing circumstances that often arise.

'We've already done a lot of preparation at the factory,'

explains senior race engineer Steve Hallam. 'There are various work lists for the jobs to be done each day – for Thursday when most of the boys get to the circuit, for Friday after practice, for Saturday after morning practice and after qualifying, and for Sunday after warm-up. At these times, fairly well-structured debriefs produce further job lists.

'All of it is made easier if the car is basically competitive, and if you have no mechanical problems or accidents you can fairly well contain your working day. If you have problems, or something that you don't understand is happening to the car, then you're eating into your sleeping time to fix it. The more in control and the more organized you are to have a normal weekend, the more time you have to deal with a problem. And that's the way we try to operate.'

thursday

Each day senior personnel attend a series of technical meetings that are usually held in a room in the West motorhome in the paddock. Scheduled to the minute, based on the 24-hour clock, the meetings are run according to a fixed format with a pre-planned agenda. The meetings held after each on-track session are called 'debriefs', though they are often not very brief at all, and over the weekend it seems as much time is spent in meetings as is spent running the cars.

The first meeting on the agenda is the Summary Meeting, where the main objectives are to finalize the car specifications for the circuit, to determine the work schedule and to

issue work lists. Those in attendance include Steve Hallam, Adrian Newey (technical director), Dave Ryan (team manager), Pat Fry and Mark Slade (race engineers respectively responsible for the cars of David Coulthard and Mika Hakkinen). Also on hand are Mike Negline (chief mechanic), and Gary Wheeler, Simon Moule and Adrian Burgess (Number One mechanics on the two race cars and the T-car).

Back at the factory, Steve and Mike have prepared job lists for each car. At the summary meeting Mike provides a situation report, going through the items on the lists to bring the engineers up to date on the state of preparation. Steve will point out special areas of concern, things to look out for on a particular circuit where the characteristics might be hard on certain components. Targets for the preparation of the race cars are set for the day, to get them mechanically finished and scrutineered. Before the cars are allowed out on the circuit they must be checked over by the FIA scrutineers to make sure they conform to the Formula 1 governing body's strict technical regulations.

In the summary meeting times are established for engine starts and pit stop practice, which will take place early in the morning. Race strategy, largely dependent on tyres and fuel loads, and already broadly mapped out in a meeting back at the factory, is also discussed. The last items on the agenda are devoted to Steve's historical quiz. The three or four questions, usually concerned with the past history of the particular event the team is currently at, are so popular that even rival teams have wished to participate.

In the Engine Meeting, representatives from Ilmor discuss with the engineers the specifications, and determine the operating parameters and schedule for the Mercedes engines that will be used over the weekend. In the Tyre Meeting, the Bridgestone engineer attached to the team reviews the previously discussed tyre plan for the weekend, including the tyre options available and their recommended usage. The Drivers' Briefing, with Mika and David, includes an explanation of the philosophy behind the set-ups chosen for their cars, possible directions to explore in pursuit of the set-ups, an outline of tyre usage and fuel load strategy, and a summary of the information available from previous races and test sessions at the circuit.

friday

Before practice begins, at 11:00hrs, there is an engine meeting to confirm the engine settings, and another meeting with Mika and David to confirm and/or update what was discussed the previous day. About 10 minutes after the first hour of practice, which ends at noon, the drivers and their engineers attend a debrief session to discuss any changes or adjustments the drivers may request on their cars. Using a circuit map, the drivers' descriptions of what their cars are doing corner by corner around the track are noted down by the engineers and compared with data from the telemetry. In this way any handling problems are identified and addressed, and the engineers are able to delve more deeply into the performance of the car and come up with any necessary changes.

The same process is repeated following the second hour of practice, which ends at 14:00hrs, though this last session of the day means there is less of a time constraint and before the debrief begins those who will attend have about 45 minutes to have a quick bite to eat. Following the debrief, in which engine performance is summarized and gear ratios are confirmed, preliminary and final job lists for the day are prepared and issued, as are a set-up sheet for Mike and the mechanics to work from, and a tyre sheet for Tats and the truckies.

Chief truckie Tats Cook controls the tyres, making sure the right rubber is available for the right car at the right time. Working with his mates Gerry Good, Forks Morrow and Drew Miller, Tats will mount and de-mount Bridgestone tyres on up to 48 sets of Enkei wheels over the weekend. The tyres are coded according to the several rubber compounds available for both wet and dry conditions (the 'wets' also come in several different tread patterns) and each set of tyres is prepared for a specific car.

'It can get complicated,' Tats admits, 'but we've done a lot of testing to make sure we're organized and don't get caught off guard under qualifying and race conditions. When the

mechanics call for another set of tyres we can issue it within 20 seconds.'

Speed is of the essence, but speed gone wrong can lead to chaos. Haste must be organized to avoid waste in an environment where the day starts quickly then speeds up. 'The goal each day,' Mike Negline says, 'is to get ourselves organized and up and running as quickly as possible, to make sure we're always one step ahead of everyone else. You've got to be on top of things and stay on top of them, right around the clock. The timetable is fairly constant at each race, but occasionally things go wrong and you've got to be prepared for emergencies.'

To perform their duties each mechanic has his own set of tools, which he buys himself and keeps spotlessly clean and arranged like gleaming surgical instruments in drawers in the three Lista cabinets (one for each car) at the back of the garage. Dealing (as they must) with oil, grease and hydraulic fluids can leave the clothing of those who work in the garage looking somewhat shop-soiled and worn. But not for long. Each morning, acting according to a document issued by Mike to ensure that everyone is similarly attired, the crew members don the fresh clothing prepared for them in the Clothing Store back at the factory.

And it's a good thing Shadwell Williams is issued with serviceable footwear. By his own definition he is 'hyperactive' and should a rare lull occur in his regular routine of running around from dawn to dusk, handing

out spares, keeping the garage spic and span, Shadwell will only slow down to a saunter.

'Once in a while I like to go on a pit walkabout, have a look around to see what the opposition is up to. So I ask Tats or Mike for permission to leave for 15 minutes or so. The problem is, as soon as I leave the garage the mechanics will need some spares out of the truck or somebody will want something. I could be here for two or three hours just polishing and cleaning, then the moment I'm gone the call will go out: "Where is he? Where is Shadwell?" So, I have to carry a radio with me every time I leave. It can be a bit of a downer, not having any time to yourself, because you're on the floor 12 hours or more every day.'

Perhaps it's just as well that Shadwell's duties don't require him to sit still through the meetings and debriefs that continue throughout the day. Between 16:00hrs and 16:30hrs there is another tyre debrief, followed by another engine meeting, which usually finishes about 19:00hrs. Some 60 minutes later, providing no major problems have been encountered, the team takes time out for a meal, provided by Lyndy Woodcock and her Absolute Taste catering staff under the canopy at the West motorhome.

'It's probably the highlight of the day,' Steve Hallam says of the evening meal, 'because it gives you a chance to communicate on a human level. We enjoy a light-hearted chat – paddock gossip, football results – general banter about subjects not necessarily to do

with racing. Dave Ryan and I are very conscious of the need to work on the human side of things, keeping up the team spirit, the morale.

'In this business you spend a lot of time in one another's company, often in some quite highly stressed situations, and therefore you really need to be able to get on with the people you are working with. You need to know when you can offer help, when to stand back, how to behave in a variety of situations. The more experience you have and the better you know them, the better-equipped you are to recognize and deal with difficulties people may be having. When someone is discouraged or suffering under the pressure, you need to let them know they are not alone.'

After the half- to three-quarter hour break for the evening meal – providing it wasn't a snack taken on the run to fortify themselves for several more hours of work – team members tidy up, leave the circuit and retire to quarters in the nearby hotels. Once in a while some of the crew will go out to a bar, have a drink and see the local sights, though the members of the 'Knitting Circle' tend to restrict their activities in this area.

According to its non-members, the Knitting Circle is composed of people like Mike Negline, Trevor Lawes and Turbo Lunnon, who are either conservative by nature or saving their money for other things – marriage, a house, a car, a holiday and so on. Some, like Derek Jeanes, float in and out of the circle, while even charter

members, such as Tats Cook, tend to stick to their knitting and call it a night not long after their long day at the circuit is over.

'You often start about five in the morning,' Tats notes, 'and you finish, if you're lucky, at eight or nine at night. So you usually want to go home pretty early. You go back to the hotel, go up to the room, start getting your stuff ready for tomorrow morning and slowly pass out.'

saturday

With the qualifying hour looming up in the afternoon, the day begins earlier and the work and the tension intensify. The first of the two 45-minute practice sessions begins at 09:00hrs, followed by a half-hour interval before the start of final practice. The team then has two hours to prepare for the start of qualifying.

While the cars are being fettled, Jerry Powell and Mark Arnall (the team's fitness specialists) continue

their work on the drivers. Jerry supervizes the overall exercise programme for both drivers, and is particularly responsible for training David. Mark, a sports physiotherapist, gives massages to both drivers and is Mika's personal trainer. As Mark puts it: 'It's our job to make sure the drivers' bodies work as efficiently as the cars.'

stress

Though Mika and David earn their living while sitting down on the job, the staggering stresses and strength-sapping situations to which their bodies are subjected make their profession one of the most physically demanding of athletes in any sport.

In the cockpit the physical stress a driver must endure begins with the muscular effort required to brace his body against the phenomenal g-forces – generated during braking, cornering and accelerating – which can literally take his breath away. Under full braking

– slowing from 315kph to 105kph in 3.5 seconds – an F1 car can generate 4.5g. In flat-out cornering the lateral forces can also reach 4.5g – four-and-a-half times the force of gravity.

The brunt of the g-force is borne by the driver's head and neck, since his head is not strapped into the cockpit like the rest of his body. The centrifugal force exerted in maximum cornering means the weight of the helmet, which has a static weight of about 1.8kg, increases to 8kg. When the weight of the driver's head is included in this equation the physical stress during cornering has been calculated to be the equivalent of the driver walking around with an 18kg weight strapped to his skull.

The physical stress on Mika and David is compounded by the constant vertical vibration from the car's rock-hard suspension pounding over the track surface. Meanwhile, a few centimetres from their backs, the howling Mercedes V10 engine causes yet more vibration, as well as hearing stress.

The normal sound of traffic on streets and roads is measured at from 60 to 70 decibels, while the assault on the eardrums created by the loudest heavy metal rock groups can reach 110 on the decibel scale. But for F1 drivers, even though it is filtered through their helmets and protective earplugs, the hullabaloo created by F1 engines measures well beyond 120 decibels, some distance past the threshold of human pain.

Another form of stress a driver must endure is thermal, which is caused by the tremendous amount of heat generated in the cramped cockpit of the car. On average, cockpit temperatures are 10 degrees C hotter than the ambient temperature of the air outside. But for the driver, cocooned in his heavy fire-retardent underwear, driving suit, shoes, gloves and helmet, the heat factor can rise as high as 50 degrees C.

While professional players exhausting themselves in the most vigorous two-hour tennis match can lose up to 2kg of their normal body weight, the F1 driver labouring in the torrid cockpit environment for about 90 minutes in a Grand Prix suffers such thermal stress that he regularly sweats off over 3kg of body weight. And after a race on a particularly hot day a driver's normal body temperature of 37 degrees C can rise dangerously high to nearly 45 degrees C.

All of these stresses, which conspire to sap a driver's strength and stamina, are compounded by the physical work he must do while driving the car. This is called energetic stress, the term used to define the muscular activity required to make steering movements and operate the foot pedals, gear shift and other cockpit controls. On average, a leverage of 15kg is required to turn the steering wheel of an F1 car, an effort made more difficult by the kickback on the

steering wheel caused by the firm suspension. Slowing down an ordinary road car under braking requires approximately 12kg of pedal pressure, but the brake pedal load required to stop an F1 car is up to 70kg.

While controlling an F1 car at speed is partly instinctive it also requires intense mental focus, which takes a physical toll. Even the relatively straightforward act of changing gears, made simpler now by the use of levers on the steering wheel, demands constant attention, particularly on tight circuits like Monaco where gear changes number almost 3,000. Each physical movement the driver makes is accompanied by half a dozen mental calculations and in total it has been estimated a driver makes up to 40,000 split-second operations during the course of a Grand Prix. Such sustained mental effort is exhausting but, since fatigue interferes with clear thinking, a driver's life can literally depend on his state of fitness.

Further depleting a driver's energy reserves are the emotional stresses that go with the job. During a race these can include aggravation while being blocked by a slower car, the exasperation occasioned by mechanical deficiencies in his machinery and so on.

There is also the need for the driver to suppress debilitating emotions such as anger over disputes with other drivers, his team, the race authorities and other such distractions. Perhaps the most tiring of all emotional conflicts for a driver is the necessity of keeping fear at bay while going fast enough to

satisfy the greatest pressure of all: to succeed.

fitness

In keeping with its relentless pursuit of racing success, McLaren leads the F1 field in matters concerning driver fitness. Jerry Powell and Mark Arnall accompany the drivers to every race and test session, and frequently work out with them in Monaco, where both Mika and David live. They also have at their disposal a new physiology laboratory at the factory in Woking, where an array of exercise equipment is used to assess the drivers' physical status and pinpoint particular areas of their bodies that need to be worked on. During race weekends, fitness headquarters is located in the back of the main motorhome, Ron's World.

'We've got a specific area in there,' Mark says, 'where we work on the drivers. It's a place where they can relax, have a shower, sit down or lie down and just concentrate. They have so many distractions during the race weekend. In the paddock, you've got thousands of people running around, fans looking for autographs, journalists wanting to talk to them. The marketing people are always after them to meet sponsors, they've got team meetings and debriefs throughout the day and so on. Whenever we can, we try and get them into the physio room and into a situation where there is as little interruption as possible.'

Jerry Powell: 'Over the weekend Mark massages each driver every evening and sometimes during the

> *"Winning is an awesome feeling, a great sense of achievement. The emotion is still sinking in as we pack up and go. Celebrating is something we don't often get a chance to do."*
> Gavin Beresford

the day as well. We train them Thursday and Friday and on Saturday evening. On Sunday morning it's mostly just loosening them up, lots of mobility exercises, lots of stretching. Working with sports nutritionist Andy Mathews, we also monitor their fluid intake and their diet over the weekend. Everything they eat and drink we write down and keep track of. At the hot weather races, they dehydrate so much that we're virtually force-feeding them drinks.

'They follow a fairly standard sports diet, 55 to 60 per cent carbohydrates, then proteins and a fairly low fat content. Our main problem is making sure they actually eat enough. It gets hard on the race weekend, where they can't really have anything to eat for two hours before they drive because the g-forces in the car will send the stuff flying around in the stomach and make them feel physically uncomfortable. So, we end up feeding them at strange times, and

making sure they get enough sleep.'

Mika would like to sleep for nine hours, but generally has less on a race weekend. 'It's sometimes difficult to relax. We do such intensive work at the track that even if I manage to get to bed at nine o'clock, my mind is still dealing with the racing when I've closed my eyes.'

David can get by with six hours sleep, but on race weekends he prefers to get a full eight hours. The training schedule devised for him by Jerry on race weekends calls for a light run early in the morning, followed by some stretching. Each day he tries to arrive at the circuit about 90 minutes before he is scheduled to drive. Those times are the highlight of DC's Grand Prix weekend.

'It's the only time that you are actually alone to do your own thing. I remember reading about drivers saying that they only really felt alive when they were behind the wheel. I now understand what they meant. I find the technical side – working with the engineers and developing the car – interesting, but what I really love is driving it. You're in there by yourself, making your own decisions. Bang! You respond to those decisions and even before

they've registered you've turned the wheel. Only in the car do I feel in control. It's a wonderful feeling. There aren't many situations in a driver's life, especially on a race weekend, where you can say that you're in complete control.'

David's team-mate talks about how nearly every minute of their weekend is programmed. 'It's absolutely planned,' Mika says, 'from Thursday right through to Sunday night, not just when you're in the car. Every day you've got meetings with the engineers and mechanics, press work, sponsor appearances.' Sometimes people think Mika never comes out of the garage or the motorhome, that he is always hiding in there. 'The reality is you have so much to do, you have no time to come out. It is very hard work indeed. Very serious business. F1 is a mind game, no question. You have to plan ahead, think ahead – out of the car and in it. In the car, if you don't keep your head in gear, the car will overtake it. There is so much to think about that sometimes smoke comes out your ears!'

engineering

Fortunately for Mika and David much of the smoke is cleared during the debrief sessions with the race engineers. In the old days, when the cars were relatively uncomplicated and easy to set up, race engineering amounted to little more than a few rudimentary suspension and wing adjustments, patting the driver on the back, helping him tighten up his seat belts and sending him out onto the track into the great unknown.

Jerry Powell (*left*) **is David's trainer. Mark Arnall looks after Mika. Their job is to make the drivers' bodies work as efficiently as their cars.**

Nowadays, much more complex technology has created many more variables so that a car's performance is dependent more than ever on the engineers working with the drivers to optimize the chassis set-up.

Steve Nichols, now on engineering duty with the Home Team but for many years the chief engineer at the races, thinks race engineers are a special breed who need to be well-equipped to do the job. 'You want somebody who's got strength of character, who isn't going to be over-awed by the occasion or the pressure. Ice water in the veins is a good characteristic to have. Being a race engineer is one of the most satisfying jobs in the pit lane.'

Under the leadership of Steve Hallam, race engineers Mark Slade and Pat Fry, and the junior engineers Phil Prew and Paul Monaghan, depend heavily on feedback from Mika and David, who must be acutely sensitive to the way the cars perform and be able to recall and interpret their impressions back to the engineers who, in turn, must be able to translate the drivers' information into the necessary chassis adjustments.

Much of the information with which the engineers work is provided by the computers that spew forth a steady stream of highly sophisticated and complex data, which has to be translated into practical engineering applications. The phenomenon of electronic information gathering, through data logging and acquisition, computer analysis and telemetry, means that the team's Embedded Systems and Data Analysis engineers never touch a spanner.

For Tyler Alexander and Paul Cann (respectively the Embedded Systems engineer and the Data Analysis technician on Mika's car), and Anton Stipinovich and Julian Chapman (their counterparts on DC's car), their most important tool is a computer, which, linked to sensors mounted on the car, monitors g-forces, suspension movements on each wheel, engine rpm, road speed, throttle position, brake pressure and so on. The data tells the engineers to the split second exactly what is happening in the car and driver combination, as well as when and where it is happening on the circuit.

Besides the need for them to be computer literate, analytical and precise, engineers must be cool-headed and able to work under fire – to function fully in the often chaotic racing environment. The outcome of a Grand Prix is often determined by the performance of the engineers – in planning race strategy and tactics, the timing of pit stops for refuelling and fresh tyres, the pacing of the driver and so on. Since qualifying performances frequently influence race results, much depends on the expertise of the engineers in preparing the cars for that vital 60-minute session that begins at one o'clock on Saturday afternoon.

qualifying

In the first nine Grands Prix of the 1998 season a West McLaren Mercedes car started from pole position in every race. In six of those races Mika and David shared the front row. According to Mika, being the quickest qualifier on six of those occasions had much to do with his level of concentration. 'It's a very big part of qualifying, and you build up to it. You have to really start maximizing your concentration on Friday, because on Saturday you have even less time to do it. In qualifying, the pressure is really on and the concentration level has to be as high, maybe even higher than in the race.'

To prepare himself for an all-out

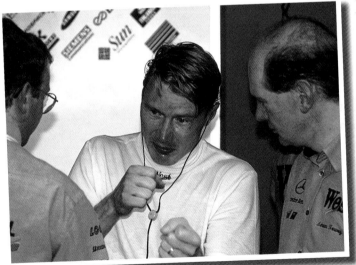

Mika says you have to keep your head in gear or the car will overtake it. Engineering solutions from Mark Slade and Adrian Newey help keep him on course.

effort in qualifying Mika retires to the motorhome with his trusted trainer. They sit in the drivers' room with the lights turned off. Mark Arnall: 'Mika sits there in the dark, in a driving position, and he talks through exactly what he's going to do for the qualifying lap. He's actually steering with his hands at the time and he talks about what speeds he's going to do on what part of the course, what gear he's going to be in, where he's going to shift down, where he's going to shift up, where he's going to brake, where he's going to accelerate – from start to finish all the way around the lap. He does four, maybe five of these mental laps. And when I ask him what time he's going to do in qualifying, he's usually been right on – to within a tenth of a second. It's quite amazing.'

David agrees with Mika that the real pressure on the drivers starts on Saturday afternoon, for what he calls a journey into the great unknown. 'Friday is more relaxed, a bit like a test day, though if you get off to a bad start in practice it can affect your whole weekend. But you've got to be completely focused for qualifying. If it's not working for you, if you're having a balance problem with the car or if you're making a mistake somewhere on the lap, it can be very frustrating. If you're having a good weekend, then that hour can be one of the most enjoyable of all, because it's really a journey into the unknown. It's the quickest lap that you've ever done around that track. You've got to push to the absolute limit, beyond where

you've been before. And you wonder what it's going to feel like. How do you know what the limit is, until you actually do it? It's a great experience, very intense.'

Shadwell Williams talks about how the intensity reaches fever pitch in the garage.

'Qualifying is very, very tense. We're all hyped up – the mechanics, the truckies, everybody is on edge. We will run around like crazy for the guys, do whatever it takes to get those cars out. The place could be swimming in oil, but it doesn't matter. If you have to run over people, you try to do it politely, but for that one hour the cars come first. When it's over, you switch back into presentation mode, tidying up, beautifying everything. And if we're on pole, and have the front row locked up the way we've been doing, the whole garage lights up. Everybody's got big smiles on their faces.'

For Steve Hallam, qualifying is a very exciting time. 'I love it. At two o'clock on Saturday afternoon, you know where you are in the pecking order, where you stand relative to the other teams. There is a release of tension. You come back into the motorhome for the debrief, and you sort of flop down, either with happiness or with disappointment.

For David, a quick qualifying lap is a journey into the great unknown. The pressure is intense, the experience sensational.

Thankfully, this year we've been flopping down with happiness.

'Being competitive, getting pole position, gives the driver a huge lift. I cannot stress how good a driver will feel going into a race day knowing that he's on pole. He knows he's got the best car, no one else can drive faster than him. It's great for the driver's confidence and it boosts everyone on the team. After a really good qualifying session the boys are over the moon.'

The moon may be rising before the boys leave the circuit on Saturday night. Forty-five minutes after qualifying there is another debrief, followed by another engine meeting, and in the garage the lights will be burning brightly until all hours.

the paddock

Meanwhile, out in the motorhome kitchens, Lyndy Woodcock and her catering staff are still firing on all burners. At the Silverstone circuit for the 1998 British Grand Prix, the team's home race, the 10 members of Lyndy's crew work with absolute haste. Their days begin at five in the morning, when they leave the nearby hotel to prepare breakfast for the Race Team. While they feast on a full English breakfast, Lyndy and company are already working on lunch for the team's guests.

Late in the afternoon Ron Dennis and Norbert Haug meet the media at the Mercedes motorhome, which becomes particularly crowded because of the interest generated by the team's front-running status. While the Mercedes press officer Wolfgang Schattling hosts this event, the head of

Bob McMurray is well qualified to keep partners and guests up to date with the action. He's been with the team for three decades.

McLaren International's media communications is in the midst of one of her busiest weekends of the year.

As Anna Guerrier says: 'I'll get to the circuit by eight in the morning to ensure that the fax, modem and computer in the motorhome are working. This is vital because each day my press releases will be faxed or e-mailed to journalists across the world, handed to 300 or so in the pressroom and sent to 100 of McLaren's partners.

'After qualifying, I'll write press releases and distribute them by hand to the journalists before dealing with driver interviews, where the journalists and TV crews fight (and I have the bruises to prove it!) to speak to Mika or David. I'm also available to answer any questions, though the ringing mobile phone will constantly interrupt these conversations, so being able to hold several conversations at once is a requirement of the job.

'Of course, Sunday is the biggest day. I'll be watching the race from the pit garage, where there will be numerous interruptions as television crews clamour for information throughout. Depending on the result of the race, it's a re-run of Saturday with a driver press conference to be attended, journalists' questions to be answered and the press release to write and distribute. As the team and our guests celebrate or commiserate,

my day will continue until the last communication is sent out to the world. It's likely to be a long haul.'

Like Anna, her TAG McLaren Marketing Services colleagues at Silverstone are as busy as their team-mates in the garage. In fact, the marketing work at Silverstone began at a test session at the circuit the week before, when 500 team guests a day, from Monday through to Friday, were shown through the garages. That was a dress rehearsal for the British Grand Prix weekend, when the guest list would number 315 people on Friday, 460 on Saturday and 497 on race day. In addition, the team's partner Mobil had invited 250 guests, with Bridgestone and Loctite having 50 guests apiece.

The interior of the team's sumptuous VIP suite in the Paddock Club at Silverstone took six men four days to set up, under the watchful eye of Bob McMurray. After the VIP suite and the motorhomes were made shipshape to his satisfaction, Bob would devote much of the rest of the weekend to keeping the guests up to date on the activities of the Race Team.

When the cars are on the track Bob is linked to the team via a headset and provides the guests with a running commentary to accompany what they see on the several large screens and approximately 20 TV sets in the suite. Having been with the team for three decades, and worked at everything from driving the transporters to wielding spanners on the cars, Bob knows what he is talking about.

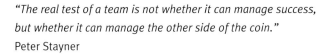

"The real test of a team is not whether it can manage success, but whether it can manage the other side of the coin."
Peter Stayner

'We think it's important to keep the weekend guests involved and well-informed about what the team is up to. We want to give them the complete race experience, along with the team. After a win, we take two magnums of champagne and spray everybody to duplicate what our drivers are up to on the podium. It's only done when we're on the top step of the podium. Second or third don't count.'

Peter Stayner, head of Partner Management at TMMS, is busy providing guests with more of the race experience. 'Every Grand Prix has its own personality, and we try to capture it for our partners and guests. We take them on tours through the garage, have the drivers talk to them, make presentations, build up the atmosphere and the excitement. Like the team, our whole weekend is programmed out to the minute.

'We don't just go through the motions. It's important that we really put the effort into it, giving our guests the kick, giving them that same buzz, all that emotion, which those of us in the team are feeling. We try to make sure that their Grand Prix weekend with us is something they will remember for the rest of their lives.'

sunday: the countdown

08:00hrs: Adrian Newey, Steve Hallam, Pat Fry and Mark Slade meet with two Ilmor engineers to confirm the engine settings.

08:30hrs: Adrian, Steve, Pat and Mark are joined by Mika and DC to outline and confirm the running programme for the 30-minute warm-up session.

09:30hrs: Warm-up.
Steve Hallam: 'All options on race strategy remain open until after warm-up. Every time you run the car, you try to learn something, and warm-up is no exception. Consequently, we treat this period as simply an extension of our race weekend programme and use the data generated to complement that already learned. The key to race performance is understanding how the tyres are going to perform over a number of laps. Starting from the front row allows a wider range of strategies to be considered and, in addition, one is mindful of where the main opposition is going to come from, relative to our drivers.'

10:15hrs: Steve, Dave Ryan and two Ilmor men hold a debrief with the drivers and their race engineers to summarize engine performance, and confirm gear ratios and the chassis set-up, after which a preliminary job sheet is issued as quickly as possible.

11:00hrs: Dave accompanies Mika and DC to the mandatory FIA Drivers' Briefing, which is attended by all the drivers.

12:00hrs: Dave and the drivers go back to the West motorhome where the team's earlier debrief session is reconvened.

12:15hrs: Ron Dennis comes into the motorhome for the Race Strategy Meeting. In this all-important meeting the race set-up for both cars is finalized, the fuel stop and tyre strategies for the cars are confirmed and a final set-up sheet is issued to the crew in the garage.

'We present our final strategy recommendations to Ron, who has kept up with developments throughout the weekend,' says Steve Hallam. 'The strategy meeting can be fairly hectic. If we're in trouble in any way it can be tainted by that. But the skill behind all this, and the reason we operate in such a structured way, is that it presents a framework for everyone to work within. You can follow the structure and you've got people in the various positions that are delegated to do the work correctly. Mike is very organized in the garage, Tats has got the tyres organized and so on. And if you're resourced in terms of manpower, and all of your equipment is working, everything will fall into place.

'There is an element of competition between the two drivers and their crews on the two cars, but we try to race as a team, not against each other. For example, the driver who qualified highest on the grid is allowed to select his strategy first. His decision as to when he wants to make his pit stop has a priority over the other driver. This is pre-determined so that there is not a fight on the pit wall when someone wants to stop, because that would be counter-productive to the team's performance. There's a lot to consider in determining strategy. It's a complex business, running a race.'

13:00hrs: An hour before the start the drivers are preparing their minds for the business at hand.

Mika, sitting quietly with Mark, is working on the mental imagery to take him over the full race distance. 'Yes, I am nervous. You just learn to control it.

A certain amount of it can be useful in the race.'

David, with his girlfriend Heidi Wichlinski sitting nearby, is lying down in the back of the motorhome. He's been racing since he was 11 years old and as a teenager, 'I was all nerves. I still find it difficult to relax if a lot of people are around, but if I can lie quietly for 15 or 20 minutes I can just switch off. I close my eyes, think about my set-up, visualize the start. Sometimes I actually fall asleep.'

13:30hrs: The pit lane opens, the cars leave the garage and assume their positions on the starting grid, where the engines are switched off and the crews perform last-minute tasks. Mika and David get out of their cars. Mark and Jerry stand beside them, making sure they drink at least half a litre of water in the next half hour.

13:45hrs: The pit lane closes. The drivers make a quick visit to the toilet. David, using his mobile phone, calls his mother and father back home in Twynholm, Scotland. 'Just going to start,' he says. 'Speak to you after the race.'

13:55hrs: The crews pack up and walk off the grid, back to the garage. Mark Slade and Mika's crew wish him good luck. Pat Fry and DC exchange a final word and Gary Wheeler, DC's Number One mechanic, gives his driver a ritual wink. 'Thank you very much, guys,' David says. 'See you at the finish.'

14:00hrs: The engines are fired up and the cars set out on the formation lap, weaving back and forth to warm up the tyres, progressing slowly around the circuit in single file to take up their positions in front of the starting lights.

Across the pit lane from the garage the personnel who will observe and direct the race put on their radio headsets and take up their positions in front of the monitors on the two timing stands set up behind the pit wall. On one stand are Norbert Haug and Mario Illien, one or two representatives from Mercedes–Benz headquarters and the team's Bridgestone tyre man. On the other timing stand are Ron Dennis, Steve Hallam, Mark Slade, Pat Fry, Adrian Newey and Dave Ryan. At one end of this stand is Gerry Good, who readies the lap board he will use to signal Mika; at the other is DC's lap board man, Gavin Beresford.

Standing in the back of the garage are Mika's wife Erja (they were married during the 1998 season) and David's girlfriend, Heidi. They've been with their men throughout the weekend and at this most critical time they want to be as close to the action as possible. 'I want to be in there with the team,' Erja says, 'where I can see from their faces whether things are going well or not. I don't want to sit in the motorhome talking to people. I'd rather be where everybody is working and totally committed. I don't think I'm particularly nervous. Excited, yes. I keep out of the way, and I must admit I love the intensity of the atmosphere.'

At the seven workstations in the back of the garage the McLaren and Ilmor data and telemetry engineers stare intently into their monitors. In the front of the garage the rest of the team waits expectantly. The 22 people who will participate in the pit stops stand in their black fireproof suits, with their balaclavas and black helmets at the ready. They are all wearing headsets but now, moments from the start, Patch Vale prepares for the moment he loves, and loves to talk about. He lifts up his headphones and just listens 'to all those cars take off! There is nothing on this earth like this moment. The sound is absolutely amazing! This is the high point of the whole weekend for me. This is why we're here. This is what it's all about!'

the race

Providing the two Mercedes V10 engines are making a major contribution to that mighty crescendo of noise at the start, the people on the timing stand heave a sigh of relief. Then – from now until the chequered flag – they think, and they wonder, and they question.

As Steve Hallam says: 'One of several peaks has passed in that they've got safely off the grid and into the first corner. Another peak is the relief at not having a red light that stops the race. There is nothing so irritating as a re-started race. And when you're under way and you've got your race plan and you know what you're going to do, there are questions you're continually asking yourself and the others. You're trying to grapple with a lot of factors. Are we on the right strategy to do the best we possibly can? Are the dynamics of the race going to dictate a change in your plans? If they are, what are you going to do about it? You're looking for gaps in the traffic. Where is your driver going to rejoin the race after his pit stop? If he's stopping in or out of phase, are you going to put him in trouble.'

Erja and Heidi wish Mika and David good luck. Win or lose, they will remain heroes.

pit stop

In the garage the members of the pit crew are watching and waiting for the moment their services will be required. Except for Shadwell Williams, who is having his customary nap on the floor, they are following the race on the overhead monitors and tuned in to the team's radio conversations. Mike Negline, the one with the nickname 'Ruby' inscribed on his protective helmet, grasps the lollipop like an orchestra conductor's baton. Standing by are the front and rear jackmen, Ian Coates and Adrian 'ATB' Burgess, who will be the first to spring into action.

The wheelmen are grouped in the four trios in which they will perform. Those on the left front wheel are the airgun operator Simon 'Simoni' Moule, Julian 'Lofty' Chaplin who will take the wheel off, and Trevor 'Trevooor' Lawes who will put the new one on. Their counterparts at the right front wheel are Gary 'Wimp' Wheeler, Shadwell and Paul 'Taff' James. Poised to pounce on the left rear wheel are John 'Johnny O' Ostrowski, Kris 'Bruv' de Groot and Chris 'Gromit' Thompson. On the right rear are Stephen 'Al' Giles, Mark 'Turbo' Lunnon and Keith 'Wingnut' Barnard.

Standing by the refuelling rig is its operator Roger 'Red' Duff, with Andrew 'Drew' Miller on the fire extinguisher. Paul 'Bass' Cann is ready to mop up any fuel spills, and also to clean out the 'rat boxes' (the air intakes on the sidepods of the car) or replace a nosecone, should that be required. Grasping the heavy fuel hose is Patch Vale, whose mate Forklift Morrow has a

firm grip on the nozzle. Also on the alert is Jo 'Señor Jo' Ramirez, who will clean the drivers' visors.

To this point in the Grand Prix weekend, pit crew members have been fully occupied with their regular duties as truckies and mechanics. Now, as their moment in the spotlight approaches, there is a collective rush of adrenaline, tempered by feelings of apprehension. 'Yes,' Wingnut Barnard confesses, 'for a few split seconds it is a very tense time. Usually, it's quite controlled, though sometimes there's a sense of panic. But you always seem to get the job done, and then stand back and laugh about it afterwards.'

For Simoni Moule, whose 'civilian job' is Mika's Number One mechanic, the tension he feels operating a wheel gun in a pit stop is one of the main attractions. 'I think it's basically why I do it. It's the most exciting part of the weekend. You just hope you don't fuck up. Touch wood, it hasn't happened to me yet. The worst part is waiting for the car to come in. You're on tenterhooks, especially if things are really close out on the track. Sometimes, I can't watch it on the monitor and just pace around the garage. I don't really want to know what is going on.'

As the Number One mechanic on the T-car 'Top Bollocks' Burgess takes pride in being able to get the spare machine ready for the road – changing the drivers' seats, the pedals, the wheels, the stickers, the set-up, as required – in eight minutes flat. But nothing beats the thrill of handling the rear jack during an eight-second pit stop. 'Your heart's

"Just listen to those cars take off! There is nothing on this earth like this moment!" Patch Vale is also thrilled that David and Mika are leading again. Backstage: Patch, Trevooor, Wingnut, Turbo and the other players in the pit stop drama await their anxious seconds in the limelight.

pumping away. The old adrenaline is right up there. You're involved and you're taking part. You're putting your little bit into the team effort.'

John Ostrowski compares the thrill of being under the gun, the one he uses on the left rear wheel, to the parachute jumps he made during his seven-year stint in the army. 'It's a similar experience because you start by being quite concerned with the whole atmosphere. Then the whole process you've trained for takes over. When a stop is coming up we get the word from Mike with about four laps to go, and we kick Shadwell awake. You're fairly relaxed until maybe two laps before the stop. Then the adrenaline kicks in. Once the car is actually coming in, you just go through the motions, and no matter how often you do it you get the biggest buzz you can possibly imagine.'

When it's time for Kris de Groot to remove the left rear wheel during a stop, he never stops to think. 'I've always thought that if you do, that's where you've lost it. You just see the car coming down the pit lane. You know what you've got to do. You've practised it a hundred times. You just get on and do it. You're part of a team of three guys around that wheel. When the car stops, Simoni takes the nut off, then I take the wheel off and shove it away through my legs. While Steve Giles is feeding on the next wheel I push the other side of it and then Simoni goes back on it with the gun. Simple, really.'

It may sound simple to the crew directly under fire but for some who are watching, those few seconds can be unnerving. Out on the pit wall Gav Beresford is busy supplying information to DC on his pit board. When Gav

flashes the signal that tells his driver its time to make a pit stop he begins to reflect on what could go wrong.

'Dare I say it, I'm always aware of the dangers involved in refuelling. I guess an element of self-preservation sets in and you begin to wonder. If the worst should happen you've got to think about making a quick exit if you can. Probably the worst thing we could do on the pit wall is to jump without looking, because you never know if you're going to land in front of an oncoming car. But I do work out an escape route before the start of the race, in case things should get nasty. Fortunately, it's never happened to us yet and our guys are just brilliant at pit stops. It's really exciting to watch them in action.'

Should Gavin's worst fears ever be realized Drew Miller, the man on the fire extinguisher, will have to respond. 'I had to put out fires when I was in the army,' says the veteran Drew, whose silver helmet identifies him as the

fireman 'but I'll be very happy if I'm never needed here. The highlight of the day for me is watching the car going down the pit lane after everything's gone well.'

Drew and his mates remember the fearful inferno that engulfed the Benetton pit a few years ago. The fire, ignited when fuel spilled onto a red hot engine, was quickly extinguished and there were no serious injuries. 'That was the scariest thing,' says Shadwell Williams. 'You shudder when you see pictures of that big one at Benetton. But you think: "Oh, it will never happen to us," because we've got really good people at the sharp end of the stick – our hoseman Patch and Forklift on the nozzle.'

'At least where I am, I can see what's going on,' says Patch Vale, 'and I'll be the first to know if any fuel is leaking. I feel quite protected, bundled up the way we are, and I'm not too worried about it. When I do get a bit nervous is when the car comes off the jacks and is sitting there on the ground with the motor revving. We're still putting fuel in and you can feel the driver pick up first gear. When he does that the car jumps forward just a little bit. When that happens, you get nervous. You wonder: "Is he going, or is he staying?"'

Whether he stays or goes will depend on the lollipop signal given by Ruby, for whom directing the pit stops is a trying time. The heavy responsibility of this crucial position is why Ron Dennis handled it for so many years and was reluctant to give it up. When Ron was finally persuaded to go back to the pit wall, the duty was given to Mike Negline whose sense of responsibility is so great that the lollipop job weighs heavily on his mind. 'I don't really enjoy it. My stomach gets tied up in knots, because of the risk. It's a very serious decision to make, to hold the car or let it go. You've got to watch for other cars coming down the pit lane. You've got to be absolutely sure all the boys are finished before you let the car go. And that is a very, very serious business, because in the end you're the one responsible for the welfare of a couple of dozen blokes.'

The bloke on the end of the fuel nozzle is Forks Morrow, on whose prowess the duration of a refuelling stop largely depends. Somehow, Forks is able to keep stress at bay and carry out his duties in a calm and methodical way. 'Maybe it's because you're so

focused on just that nozzle and the digital lights that come on when the fuel rig is empty. There might be other things going on that you should worry about, but you don't really see anything else. You just concentrate completely on what you're doing. Obviously, you feel a bit of added pressure in situations like we had at Monza that time, when David came in for his stop right behind Alesi's Benetton, which was in the lead. We needed to be really sharp and get David out in front, which we did. So that was a good feeling.'

That race, the 1997 Italian Grand Prix, was arguably Forklift's finest hour, and the whole team loves him for it. Alas, poor Forklift was also the focus of attention in a pit stop that went wrong, when the nozzle refused to engage on the adaptor of the fuel tank of DC's car. Forks remembers that day, at the 1998 French Grand Prix, as 'probably the worst time of my life at McLaren, to be honest. It is a day I would like to forget. David was on course for a high finish, maybe even a win, and all he wound up with was sixth place. I did take it personally, because at the end of the day I'm the last link in the chain. In that situation my performance, although it was a mechanical problem, cost a loss of performance for the

Patch on the hose and Forklift on the nozzle are at the sharp end of the refuelling stick.

whole team. We were in a battle with Ferrari and they were closing the gap, so the last thing we needed was an error in refuelling.'

Once Forks and the rest of Mike's blokes have speedily done their good work the ball is back in the court of the 'Prats' Perch' people across the pit lane. On the timing stand Pat Fry and Dave Ryan are masterminding DC's race, while Mark Slade and Steve Hallam are running Mika, and Ron Dennis is looking at the big picture.

'Ron is observing everything,' says Steve Hallam, 'taking an overview of our cars, but also looking at the whole race. Mika doesn't like a lot of chitchat on the radio. He prefers to concentrate on what he's doing, so we feed him only what he needs to know. David talks a lot during the race to Pat and Dave. There is information coming to us from a lot of places, not just the drivers. You've got input from the data coming in steadily, and then you've got your own view of what's happening. And you make the call and the judgements as you see fit.

'A race can be the fastest hour-and-three-quarters you can ever, ever imagine. The only time when the minutes seem to slow down is when you're leading. When you're in front you want the time to pass faster. Whenever you're not leading you really want time on your side. The most difficult time is when you've got yourself into a situation where you can win, and you can see it coming, then something stops you from doing it. Then, you get very tired.'

finish line

'You get to the end of the race, and you have a brief period as everything settles down to react to what's happened,' Steve Hallam explains. 'If you've done well, then it's wonderful and everyone is joyous. If you've retired or it's been appalling, you come into the garage and kick something. The important thing is to speak to the boys after the race, congratulating them or commiserating with them, as the case may be.'

More often than not as the 1998 season unfolded congratulations were in order. When commiserations were necessary they were only a small comfort to some. Defeat does not rest lightly on the shoulders of the likes of Mike Negline, who comes close to sharing the physical pain Ron Dennis famously feels after not winning.

'The whole point of the weekend is winning the race,' according to Mike's philosophy. 'Generally, I think that if you don't come first or second, there's no point in going racing. So I am fairly well disappointed if we don't do well, because I feel that with McLaren we have everything we need to do the business – the size of the company, the facility, the technology, the back-up, the personnel. If we don't finish a race the way we should, we just have to put our heads down, work harder than ever and get the job done the next time.'

As Mika and David attend a final debrief with the engineers, and Mike and the mechanics pack up, and Tats and the truckies load the transporters in preparation for the long haul back to Woking, the team manager Dave Ryan is in a reflective mood. 'The race is almost history before it's over. The truckies are working flat out, the engineers and mechanics are already looking towards the next race, the drivers to the next test. You have to perform well at this race, you have to perform well at the next one, it's a continuous cycle of very hard work.

'Win or lose, we have to go on. We are here to win and the plus side of winning is when you look in the garage and see it on the faces of the guys. It's the same when we get back to the factory. Everybody is on a high and it makes it that much easier to do what has to be done in the days ahead.'

The pit wall barely restrained the team's joy as Mika's car shrieked over the finish line in the streets of Monaco. But David's car was silent.

the results

Seven times in the first part of the 1998 season the team enjoyed the thrill of victory. In the other four races, after being in a position to win, the team suffered the agony of defeat. At one race, the Monaco Grand Prix, the pendulum swung between both ends of the emotional spectrum.

From their first and second positions on the starting grid Mika and David took control and were running away with the famous race through the streets of Monte Carlo, the one that puts an F1 team and its sponsors into the limelight more than any other event on the calendar. On the West McLaren Mercedes timing stands the mood was euphoric, though that mood was leavened by a sense of apprehension that would prove to be partly well-founded.

Steve Hallam: 'When you put the two cars on the front of the grid at Monaco, and have both drivers race one another at this very unpredictable place where the barriers can leap out at you and so many things can go wrong, it is a very special achievement. We were leaving the rest of the field behind and a really good scrap between our two guys was in the making. Then, after 18 laps, David's engine let go, and from that point we were just hanging on mentally, supporting Mika.

'We didn't know what David's problem was and it is this lack of knowledge that turns you inside out. Once you understand the problem, you can deal with it. But

we didn't know if Mika might have a similar problem, and everybody who was up there on the stand was going through the most terrible emotions. It seemed to go on and on and on. The tension takes a physical toll on your body, standing there, taking all the notes down, getting the signals right, and steeling yourself for what might happen, wondering whether the feelings that were welling up inside would culminate in a victory or be wiped out at a stroke at any second. When we climbed down off that stand after Mika won, we were shattered, completely drained.'

The deeper their understanding of the technical complexity of the machinery, the greater the apprehension and anxiety for some members of the team. When chief designer Neil Oatley is not at a race he watches it on television at home, or listens to it on the radio. 'Listening to it gives you a different perspective,' Neil believes. 'You're using your imagination to flesh out the picture, to understand what's happening. So a couple of races a year I like to listen to the radio, and then watch the re-run on TV in the evening. That's another interesting way of soaking up the atmosphere.

'But one of the horrors of being so closely involved with the car is you're constantly going through what might break or be worried that something has been incorrectly designed, the fear of throwing it all away for some mistake. If something hasn't gone right and you feel you could have influenced it in a different way, you obviously feel a lot of

pressure within yourself, but there isn't any pressure on you from the team. I have to say that Ron is very good at not pointing the finger at anyone or trying to off-load the blame to any individual. If we are in trouble everyone pulls together to try and make it right. And, equally, if we're successful, it's shared by all the people.'

Still, the sharing factor that is emphasized by the team does not prevent certain of its members from feeling personally responsible when things go wrong. Among them is the head of Aerodynamics, Henri Durand. 'We are among the best-funded Formula 1 teams, with everything we need to be first, the best. Second is not good enough. And here I am among a very small group of people who are responsible for its success or failure on the technical side. Effectively, that is a very flattering position to be in. But we have no excuses to fail and as a consequence, when it fails, you just take it out on yourself. The bottom line is that when we have failed I must admit part of it is down to me.'

When Mario Illien climbed down off the timing stand after watching that Monaco Grand Prix in which Mika won and David did not finish, he was experiencing a conflict of emotions. One of the Mercedes V10 engines had been victorious, the other had failed. No one is more aware than Mario how difficult it is to design a racing engine capable of winning, let alone finishing a race, and when one of his engines fails to go the distance no one feels the pain more deeply.

'I sometimes wish I could drill a hole in the ground and disappear completely. You try to control your emotions, but I think a competitive person is competitive partly because of his emotions. When things go badly you can definitely feel your heartbeat go up; you get tense and you feel really low. It can be difficult, and at those times I prefer to be just left alone rather than be among people.'

On a Grand Prix weekend it is Peter Stayner's job to be among the team's partners and corporate guests, and sometimes having the painful duty of explaining to them what went wrong. 'Imagine what that's like. You've got everybody there – the company chairman, the directors, all the people that matter are your guests. And when you don't get a good result it hurts. It

At Monaco, Steve, Adrian, Ron and Dave ran an emotional gauntlet, experiencing both the thrill of victory and the agony of defeat. It left them shattered.

really hurts. We are in an emotional business. But we just have to control those emotions because the guy who has put his money into the team is probably more disappointed than you, if that's possible.

'We have to manage that and make sure we're absolutely honest. If a gearbox goes, it goes. When an engine has blown, it's blown. Period. Mario, Ron and Norbert are honest about it and explain that when you're pushing development, trying so hard to win, these things can happen. The partners appreciate that honesty and the fact that we don't try to cover up mistakes.'

Inevitably, drivers pushing to the limit sometimes go beyond it, and when that happens David is forthright about it. 'If I make a mistake I will say, "Sorry about that," and apologize to

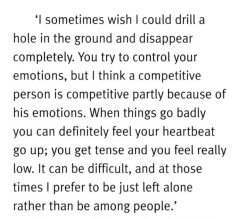

the team. It tends to weigh on me, and there is a feeling of guilt. If I hit a barrier or lose the car in a gravel trap, I can usually work out what I did wrong, but I worry about what the others think of me. I don't like to imagine them thinking: "That guy has done it again." And I like to feel that they forgive me for the mistake.'

The ever-present fear of a mistake resulting in harm to a driver is too much for some on the team to bear. Ray Grant, who spent several years with the Race Team and is now production control manager in the Home Team, hasn't been to a Grand Prix since 1980. 'The guys on the team are always

saying, "You should come to a test. You should come to a race, just to see what it's like." But I find I'm not a good spectator. In my day, I saw a few people get killed. That leaves a scar, and you hope to hell that it doesn't happen very often. It's much safer now, but Formula 1 still has that element to it. You do your bit to make a car as reliable as you can, and you rely on the driver to do his bit. But for me, the spectating, and the waiting each time they come around, is too nerve-wracking.'

F1 drivers are supposed to have nerves of steel and to perform to their maximum behind the wheel they must keep their emotions at bay. But on at least two occasions the depth of feeling experienced by both Mika and David has caught them by surprise. He never expected it, and it was the first time it happened in the 15 years of his racing career, but David wept when he won the opening race of the 1997 season, the Australian Grand Prix in Melbourne. 'It was partly for myself, because it was over a year since I'd won, with Williams. And it was partly for the team, because it was the first win for the team in three years. That length of time, when you know the winning tradition of this team, is something that weighs heavily on your mind. I knew the pressure that the team and Mercedes were under, and as a result there was pressure on me. It was a great relief to win. It was put into perspective when I came back to the garage and saw how happy everyone was.'

The victory, the 105th for McLaren, was the first for Mercedes in F1 since

One–two results are most satisfying for the victors, especially when Ferrari is the vanquished. Mika and David with Michael Schumacher in Spain, 1998.

the 1955 Italian Grand Prix. To celebrate the occasion, David dyed his hair silver, acting on a suggestion that had been put to him by one of the team's most passionate players, Norbert Haug.

One of Norbert's youthful enthusiasms was rock music and, he reveals, he once aspired to being a rock star, playing piano or drums in a group like the Rolling Stones, or The Beatles. Norbert had the long hair and he knew all the songs, and he might still like to perform on stage as a hobby, just for the fun of it. On Grand Prix weekends he is noted for his dynamic leadership of post-race celebrations, that can last long into a Sunday night at the Mercedes motorhome in the paddock. It's important, Norbert believes, to be able to let your hair down after a hard-fought race that has been won – or lost.

'If we lose I think it's important that you have 20 minutes or half an hour in the motorhome and really try to relax. There is no point in suffering. If you are suffering and show yourself being destroyed, it's certainly not the right way to go forward. You cannot change the result from that Sunday, so there is nothing worse than losing much time over it. You have to make an analysis of the problem and put all your effort into making sure it doesn't happen again.

'When we win, I must say this is one of the major forces for me. I want to get that feeling and I think it is important to show you enjoy it. And let me tell you that Ron, even though he is not shouting and screaming, is deeply, deeply enjoying it. I like to lead some cheering after a win and really start the

celebration. If you cannot celebrate, you are missing something. You should celebrate and we certainly do that.'

Mika had to wait for 96 races before celebrating his first Grand Prix victory, and when it came, at Jerez in Spain in the last race of 1997, 'I just did not know what to do. Coming into the pits after the race, I was still not sure I had really won. I had to look Ron in the eye and say: "Ron, did I win or not?" I had already thought about how to stand on the podium after my first Formula 1 win. But when it happened, seven years later, I didn't know where to look, what to hear, what to say. I was in another land, outer space. It was so difficult to focus my mind. In the press room after, I couldn't say anything. I was just staring like an idiot, because it was such a superb feeling!'

Once Mika had experienced his first win he was off and running with David.

In the races early in 1998 they dominated, giving the team five one–two finishes. These results had a profound effect on everyone, including Shadwell Williams. 'It was simply unbelievable! There was just no way I could have my little sleep in the garage, waiting for the pit stops, at those races. It was awesome. I just couldn't shut off. I stood there with the other guys, watching it all happen on the monitor – just watching Mika and David go. It was brilliant!'

Mika Hakkinen: 'Once you get that winning feeling, you want it more and more. And the team gets that feeling, too. Everybody works harder. It's teamwork, and everybody's working together. So, at the end of the day, we're all winners.'

Ron Dennis: 'We're here to win. Nothing else counts. Being second is first of the losers.'

The record: McLaren's record in F1 racing

(to the end of the 1997 season)

"Statistics give a very dry account of the McLaren story. They scarcely convey the three decades of human effort and technological achievement that this anniversary represents. The McLaren story is made of the greatest highs and the greatest lows in motor racing. However, the dedication of all the people involved in the team over the years has remained unaltered through thick and thin, and I would like to take this opportunity to thank them all for their contribution."

RON DENNIS (on McLaren's 30th anniversary, 1996)

Grand Prix seasons: 32; Grands Prix contested: 460; Grand Prix victories: 107; Pole Positions: 80; Fastest Laps: 71; Drivers' World Championships: 9; Constructors' World Championships: 7

9 Drivers' World Championships

1974: Emerson Fittipaldi

1976: James Hunt

1984: Niki Lauda

1985: Alain Prost

1986: Alain Prost

1988: Ayrton Senna

1989: Alain Prost

1990: Ayrton Senna

1991: Ayrton Senna

7 Constructors' World Championships

1974: McLaren M23 Ford

1984: McLaren MP4/2 TAG Porsche Turbo

1985: McLaren MP4/2B TAG Porsche Turbo

1988: McLaren MP4/4 Honda Turbo

1989: McLaren MP4/5 Honda

1990: McLaren MP4/5B Honda

1991: McLaren MP4/6 Honda

107 Grand Prix Victories

1968: Bruce McLaren: Belgium
Denny Hulme: Italy, Canada

1969: Denny Hulme: Mexico

1972: Denny Hulme: South Africa

1973: Denny Hulme: Sweden
Peter Revson: Great Britain, Canada

1974: Denny Hulme: Argentina

Emerson Fittipaldi: Brazil, Belgium, Canada

1975: Emerson Fittipaldi: Argentina, Great Britain
Jochen Mass: Spain

1976: James Hunt: Spain, France, Germany, Holland, Canada, USA East

1977: James Hunt: Great Britain, USA East, Japan

1981: John Watson: Great Britain

1982: John Watson: Belgium, USA East
Niki Lauda: USA West, Great Britain

1983: John Watson: USA West

1984: Alain Prost: Brazil, San Marino, Monaco, Germany, Holland, Europe, Portugal
Niki Lauda: South Africa, France, Great Britain, Austria, Italy

1985: Alain Prost: Brazil, Monaco, Great Britain, Austria, Italy
Niki Lauda: Holland

1986: Alain Prost: San Marino, Monaco, Austria, Australia

1987: Alain Prost: Brazil, Belgium, Portugal

1988 Alain Prost: Brazil, Monaco, Mexico, France, Portugal, Spain, Australia
Ayrton Senna: San Marino, Canada, USA East, Great Britain, Germany, Hungary, Belgium, Japan

1989: Alain Prost: USA, France, Great Britain, Italy
Ayrton Senna: San Marino, Monaco, Mexico, Germany, Belgium, Spain

1990: Ayrton Senna: USA, Monaco, Canada, Germany, Belgium, Italy

1991: Ayrton Senna: USA, Brazil, San Marino, Monaco, Hungary, Belgium, Australia
Gerhard Berger: Japan

1992: Ayrton Senna: Monaco, Hungary, Italy
Gerhard Berger: Canada, Australia

1993: Ayrton Senna: Brazil, Europe, Monaco, Japan, Australia

1997: David Coulthard: Australia, Italy Mika Hakkinen: Europe

The Race Winning Drivers

Ayrton Senna 35
Alain Prost 30
James Hunt 9
Niki Lauda 8
Denny Hulme 6
Emerson Fittipaldi 5
John Watson 4
Gerhard Berger 3
David Coulthard 2
Peter Revson 2
Mika Hakkinen 1
Jochen Mass 1
Bruce McLaren 1

The 80 Pole Positions

Ayrton Senna 46
James Hunt 14
Alain Prost 10
Gerhard Berger 4
Emerson Fittipaldi 2
Mika Hakkinen 1
Denny Hulme 1
Peter Revson 1
Keke Rosberg 1

The 71 Fastest Laps

Alain Prost 24
Ayrton Senna 12
Niki Lauda 8

Gerhard Berger 7
Denny Hulme 6
James Hunt 5
John Watson 3
Jochen Mass 2
David Coulthard 1
Emerson Fittipaldi 1
Mika Hakkinen 1
John Surtees 1

The 38 McLaren Drivers

1966: Bruce McLaren
1967: Bruce McLaren
1968: Bruce McLaren, Denny Hulme
1969: Bruce McLaren, Denny Hulme, Derek Bell
1970: Bruce McLaren, Denny Hulme, Andrea de Adamich, Dan Gurney, Peter Gethin, Nanni Galli
1971: Denny Hulme, Peter Gethin, Jackie Oliver, Mark Donohue, David Hobbs
1972: Denny Hulme, Peter Revson, Brian Redman, Jody Scheckter
1973: Denny Hulme, Peter Revson, Jody Scheckter, Jacky Ickx
1974: Denny Hulme, Emerson Fittipaldi, Mike Hailwood, David Hobbs, Jochen Mass
1975: Emerson Fittipaldi, Jochen Mass
1976: James Hunt, Jochen Mass
1977: James Hunt, Jochen Mass,

	The Cars	The Engines
Gilles Villeneuve, Bruno Giacomelli	1966: M2B	1966: Ford, Serenissima
1978: James Hunt, Patrick Tambay, Bruno Giacomelli	1967: M4A, M5A	1967: BRM
1979: Patrick Tambay, John Watson	1968: M5A, M7A	1968: Ford
1980: John Watson, Alain Prost, Stephen South	1969: M7B, M9A 4WD, M7C	1969: Ford
1981: John Watson, Andrea de Cesaris	1970: M14A, M7D, M14D	1970: Ford
1982: John Watson, Niki Lauda	1971: M14A, M19A	1971: Ford
1983: John Watson, Niki Lauda	1972: M19A, M19C	1972: Ford
1984: Niki Lauda, Alain Prost	1973: M19C, M23	1973: Ford
1985: Niki Lauda, Alain Prost, John Watson	1974: M23	1974: Ford
1986: Alain Prost, Keke Rosberg	1975: M23	1975: Ford
1987: Alain Prost, Stefan Johannson	1976: M23, M26	1976: Ford
1988: Alain Prost, Ayrton Senna	1977: M23, M26	1977: Ford
1989: Alain Prost, Ayrton Senna	1978: M26	1978: Ford
1990: Ayrton Senna, Gerhard Berger	1979: M26, M28, M28B, M28C, M29	1979: Ford
1991: Ayrton Senna, Gerhard Berger	1980: M29C, M30	1980: Ford
1992: Ayrton Senna, Gerhard Berger	1981: M29C, MP4, M29F	1981: Ford
1993: Ayrton Senna, Michael Andretti, Mika Hakkinen	1982: MP4/1B	1982: Ford
1994: Mika Hakkinen, Martin Brundle, Philippe Alliot	1983: MP4/1C, MP4/1E	1983: Ford, TAG Porsche Turbo
1995: Mika Hakkinen, Mark Blundell, Nigel Mansell, Jan Magnussen	1984: MP4/2	1984: TAG Porsche Turbo
1996: Mika Hakkinen, David Coulthard	1985: MP4/2B	1985: TAG Porsche Turbo
1997: Mika Hakkinen, David Coulthard	1986: MP4/2C	1986: TAG Porsche Turbo
1998: Mika Hakkinen, David Coulthard	1987: MP4/3	1987: TAG Porsche Turbo
	1988: MP4/4	1988: Honda Turbo
	1989: MP4/5	1989: Honda
	1990: MP4/5B	1990: Honda
	1991: MP4/6	1991: Honda
	1992: MP4/6B, MP4/7A	1992: Honda
	1993: MP4/8	1993: Ford
	1994: MP4/9	1994: Peugeot
	1995: MP4/10A, MP4/10B, MP4/10C	1995: Mercedes
	1996: MP4/11A, MP4/11B	1996: Mercedes
	1997: MP4/12	1997: Mercedes
	1998: MP4/13	1998: Mercedes

acknowledgements

Much teamwork was involved in creating this book. I would like to thank all the team-mates at McLaren for their help, with special thanks to Ron Dennis for giving the project his blessing, and to Anna Guerrier, Steve Hallam, Bob McMurray, Mike Negline, Dave Ryan, Peter Stayner, Justine Blake and Neil Trundle. For their help I am also indebted to Mario Illien and Paul Morgan at Ilmor, and to Norbert Haug and Wolfgang Schattling at Mercedes–Benz.

Background information for the book was found in written material supplied by McLaren, including its monthly publication *Racing Line*. Chief among other reference works consulted were Haymarket Publishing's magazines: *Autosport*, *Autocar* and *Motor Sport*. For research assistance thanks is owed to Peter Dick, Paul Harmer and Dan Knutson.

Gerald Donaldson

Gerald Donaldson with Ron Dennis.

picture credits

l=left, r=right, cl=centre left, cr=centre right, t=top, b=bottom.

Action Plus Photographic: 156. Agence D.P.P.I: 215. Diana Burnett: 76, 192. JF Galeron: 88l, 145, 154b, 170, 189. Gorys: 44, 135, 168, 177, 179, 183, 207. Darren Heath: 5r, 85, 95, 137, 202. Hock Zwei: 89, 144, 151 all, 152, 173; Tap 160, 194, 210. LAT: 96cr, 96r, 193, 195; Charles Coates 8, 20; Martyn Elford 166; Steven Tee 17, 115, 128, 224. Pamela Lauesen: 82, 171, 181. McLaren International Ltd/Zooom Photographic Ltd: 5l, 14, 15, 19, 31, 33, 34, 36, 37 all, 38, 41 all, 42 all, 43 all, 45, 47, 49, 50, 56, 59, 61, 62, 63, 65, 66, 67, 77, 96l, 108, 113, 116, 119, 122, 130, 132, 140, 154t, 155, 180, 200. Mercedes–Benz/Wilhelm: 98, 121, 196, 199. Y Okazaki: 29, 107, 109, 162, 169. RW Schlegelmilch: 23, 51, 57, 104, 110, 126, 147, 158, 172. Nigel Snowdon: 71, 73, 96cl, 97 all, 161. Sporting Pictures (UK) Ltd: 18, 69, 87, 100, 138, 148, 150, 164, 175, 178, 182, 186. Sutton Motorsport Images: 2, 3, 4, 7, 9, 25, 81, 88r, 91, 93, 106, 112, 134, 143, 159, 174, 184 all, 185, 190, 221, 205, 208, 209, 212, 213, 214 all, 216, 218, 219; Collins 11; Lawrence 13, 54. Racing Line: 27, 53. Bryn Williams: 101, 103, 124.

The creative team: *Editorial* – Chris Stone (CollinsWillow) and Sandra Stafford; *Design* – Arthur Brown and Tish Mills.